MW00593832

For my children and theirs.

Always Enough

A GLOBAL FOOD MEMOIR

Annette Anthony

Skyhorse Publishing

Copyright © 2024 by A. A. Anthony

All rights reserved. No part of this book may be reproduced in any manner without the express written consent of the publisher, except in the case of brief excerpts in critical reviews or articles. All inquiries should be addressed to Skyhorse Publishing, 307 West 36th Street, 11th Floor, New York, NY 10018.

Skyhorse Publishing books may be purchased in bulk at special discounts for sales promotion, corporate gifts, fund-raising, or educational purposes. Special editions can also be created to specifications. For details, contact the Special Sales Department, Skyhorse Publishing, 307 West 36th Street, 11th Floor, New York, NY 10018 or info@skyhorsepublishing.com.

Skyhorse® and Skyhorse Publishing® are registered trademarks of Skyhorse Publishing, Inc.®, a Delaware corporation.

Visit our website at www.skyhorsepublishing.com.

10 9 8 7 6 5 4 3 2 1

Library of Congress Cataloging-in-Publication Data is available on file.

Cover design by David Ter-Avanesyan

Cover photo credit: Getty Images

ISBN: 978-1-5107-7779-8
Ebook ISBN: 978-1-5107-7787-3

Printed in the United States of America.

CONTENTS

INTRODUCTION

When I began writing this book, it was for my two sons to use in their lives and to offer them a glimpse of me before I became their "maman." Now, I have one who can do so. In striving to temper the bitter with the sweet, this book holds my love for them both and those no longer with me. It is a way for me to make sense of unspeakable pain, phenomenal love, and my journey thus far.

****

The contents of my spice drawer are the sum of many journeys, my memory box, and a life's emotions. *Always Enough* is a cookbook with stories from my life. It embodies a feeling, an ethos, that what's mine at the table is ours. I am a neighborhood girl who got to know the world and connected with it through food. I lived the cliché of marrying a prince, living in Paris, London, Abidjan, New York, and Miami, and traveling globally. But clichés don't spare you coups d'état, or illness, or divorce, or any of the wounds of life. Learning about new cultures through culinary practices has been my ballast throughout all of the changes I have experienced.

All of the recipes are offered in the spirit of adapting, improvising, and preserving. They touch on many cuisines and are an amalgam of my versions of the wonderful foods, flavors, and dishes enjoyed throughout my travels, and by family, friends, and myself in good and challenging times. My mission is to share my passion for the feel, smell, taste, and meaning of what we eat.

On the practical side, while the recipes are detailed, they are easy to follow and make. You will find a cornucopia of vegetables as well as meat and fish dishes. My wish is that everyone who turns these pages will enjoy what I hope is good food inspired by my journey and will come to share the view that at the intersection of food and culture, there is always enough.

My early steps at home in the United States opened my palate and instilled the mantra of "waste not want not." My openness to the world and its flavors was a part of my DNA and was nurtured around my grandparents' dining table in Philadelphia. Growing up, I had no identifiable interest in cooking. Later in life, I would discover that I drew a good amount of encouragement and confidence from the variety of cooking I experienced as a child at home. An open palate was a very good thing, because once I left home as a young adult, life took me to places where this would come in handy.

My experience in Europe heightened my awareness of quality husbandry and the flavor of nature, while life in Africa elevated my skill at seasoning and developing my own signature taste. Always the new arrival, the foreigner, unsure of how to love, I learned how to cook. Life in England, where I now reside, propelled me to stir all of my culinary and cultural influences together.

On offer are recipes inspired by dishes sampled in Europe, from Paris's traiteurs to cozy seaside bistros in places like Biarritz, and many of the comforting delights of road trips through Italy, Spain, and Greece, which have become staples.

Gourmet Africa is reflected in dishes such as grilled peppery lemon chicken from Senegal and couscous made from the memory of a home-cooked feast in Casablanca. Everything I have had the good fortune to learn about food from chefs and home cooks who rejoice in the gathering around the prepared meal is bundled here. By remembering, I hope to show that the similarities across cultures stand out just as much as their uniqueness.

The stories and recipes begin in Philadelphia and the United States before setting off to France, my first port of call, and Europe. They continue with my move to West Africa, with the book ending with my move to England and what was cooked here.

Part 1
THE UNITED STATES

RENO STREET

Pop-pop's La-Z-Boy recliner had place of honor in the sitting room, right near the porch window. While I knew Pop-pop's recliner was his chair for reading, snacking on his peanuts, and being the head of the house, to me, it was the holding chair. He held each newborn grandchild there with the others leaning in around him to see the new baby and smile for the photo. Even Great-Granddad, Nana's father, held the babies there. It is also where Pop-pop held me when I needed soothing or shoe tying or pretended to read his newspaper with him.

I rarely sat on the sofa. Its heavy floral pattern was protected with plastic slipcovers to keep the fabric stain-free and to extend its life. Those plastic covers felt like glue on my lotioned hands and legs; they were so uncomfortable. All special photos were taken on that sofa, and whenever I took a picture with both Nana and Pop-pop, it was there we sat. Those were the days Nana would dress up, make up her face and hair, put on her pearl necklace, and smile.

My spot was the armchair next to the bookcase holding the *Encyclopedia Britannica*, atlas, and magazines. I regularly leafed through the pages of the atlas, especially the flags. Pop-pop and my father would read to me about the countries they had worked in or visited. All questions I asked were answered with reference to the pages of the encyclopedia. My mother would show me the countries where all of my gifts came from. I couldn't yet read, but the feel and smell of the pages and their colorful images are etched in my sensory memory. Those pages made the world my horizon.

An arched opening on the far side of the sitting-room wall opened to the dining table. Beyond the wall of the dining room was the family kitchen. In the dining room, Pop-pop and Nana had an ample oval cherrywood table with eight matching Chippendale chairs. A heavy display cabinet occupied the back wall. Our family was tall, so we needed a strong table for comfort. It seemed vast. Even skinny, six-year-old me had to squeeze behind the chairs to pass on the display cabinet side if someone was seated at the table.

These four walls of our living space held the aromas of the lightest toast, the sweet steam of each season's vegetables, every catch brought back from the shore. Wherever one was sat or occupied, aromas mingled in the backdrop. I imagine that layers of culinary DNA make up the wall particles!

Beyond a swinging door in the room's farthest corner, Nana's kitchen was small in foot space and big on output. A small, square, Formica-top table with steel trim and cold metal legs was pushed up to a wall. Nana and I loved the occasional light breakfast of jam-topped English crumpets or buttery Southern corn muffins and tea. Sat on Nana's lap, we both smiled down at the melting butter before taking our first bites.

Around the Table

Nana loved having everyone over for dinner on any day, but especially Sundays, holidays, special occasions, and birthdays. Among the extended family, her home was the preferred gathering place.

At mealtime, everyone except the chef—usually Nana— was seated at the table. We were rarely fewer than nine for a meal. My mother, father, brother, and I were often joined by any one of Nana's siblings and their family, and Uncle Elvis. Uncle Elvis was my father's younger brother. His name was Donald, but because of his affinity for slick hair, sports cars, tight pants, the new pop music, a smiley smirk that made him look cool, and a la dolce vita attitude, he reminded me of Elvis Presley—although my mother may have said Sam Cooke. His usual greeting was an art of inflection. Approvingly, he would cock his head and say, "Look at you! You doin' good." Or, with hand-on-shoulder concern, he would ask, "You doin' good?"

My mother enjoyed food just as much as everyone else, but you would not know that by her small frame. Having "the look" mattered to her. Lipstick and eyebrow pencil that doubled to shade her beauty spot were daily routines. My mother was ecstatic when the English model Twiggy came along. Finally, an icon, unlike curvaceous Marilyn Monroe, who made her feel normal.

Busy and pleasant, quiet and meticulous, my mother's uncle took it upon himself to invite her to a party, where she met my father. My father, born in 1940 and raised in the house on Reno Street, was a dutiful son. He realized the ambitions of a life denied his father. Dad would do what Pop-pop could not by becoming an officer in the Navy and a surgeon. Although Dad was never to be found in the kitchen, he made two exceptions for a few special dishes he had learned along his travels. One was at Christmas to make Yorkshire pudding with beef drippings, a recipe he picked up during his time ashore in Scotland. His other moment in the kitchen was during New England lobster season, steaming them with some Old Bay seasoning.

Nana's sister Doris, perfectly coiffed and suited with strands of pearls and gemstones, her husband Jay, and little Earl, were most often in attendance. Little Earl was Aunt Doris's son with Big Earl, and he wasn't little. Aunt Doris was devoted to loving looks, crafts, and always kept me busy with knitting and home craft projects. I adore her.

Every meal was an occasion; when the wait was over, dishes came to the table in style. Nana's bright white coconut cake, half my height it seemed, apple dumplings, succotash when corn and lima beans were in season, Pop-pop's catch of the day—panfried perfection—and his curry all inform my fondest memories. The seasonality of fruits and vegetables was a source of anticipation that I miss today.

The dish that brought the most pleasure to everyone and was news when it was in the making was Pop-pop's chicken curry. During World War II, Pop-pop had been a ship's cook in the U.S. Navy. He was stationed in Europe, particularly Italy, and on ships in the Pacific Ocean. Pop-pop brought the flavors from that period of his life back home with him. And he certainly was the one to encourage me to taste unfamiliar foods. So, while Nana usually did all of the cooking at Reno Street, having Pop-pop in the kitchen was an event.

Throughout the day, as the unusual smells floated out of the kitchen, whenever someone came in the house and curled up their nose at the peculiar lingering aromas, there would be a voice to explain with pride that "Pop-pop is making his curry."

The first aroma was of the chicken and butter coming from the oven. This was punctuated later in the day with the pungency of boiled eggs and the sweet earthiness of toasting coconut. Another layer of anticipation followed as the house would welcome aromas not so familiar to us for a savory dish: ground cumin, turmeric, and cardamom, all mixed with cinnamon and other spices I couldn't identify. Somehow the butter smell captured all of the aromas to create a warm and spicy feeling. When we were called to the table, the condiments were already there, each with its own dish and spoon. We would sit until the curried chicken and rice appeared around the corner of the kitchen door and welcome it with eager gasps.

Here in this hearth in 1960s West Philadelphia lay the roots of my own love of cultures, travel, and food. To this day, making curry takes me back to our West Philadelphia row home and our family table with everyone around me.

LAMB CURRY
Start to finish: 2½ hours
Serves 4

6 lamb neck fillets cut into cubes

1 large yellow onion, halved and thinly sliced
1 cup water
1 small bunch of chopped coriander/cilantro leaves
1 tomato, deseeded and chopped
2 tablespoons tomato paste

Curry Marinade
Mix the following together in a large bowl:

2 cups nonfat Greek yogurt
3 heaping teaspoons curry powder
2 teaspoons turmeric
2 teaspoons garam masala
1 teaspoon chili powder
3 teaspoons salt
1 heaping teaspoon ground ginger or fresh slivers
¼ cinnamon stick
6–8 cardamom pods (hit with mallet to open up a bit)
6 black peppercorns
2 teaspoons cumin powder
125g/8 tablespoons butter
Heavy cream

Add the lamb to the curry marinade. Cover and refrigerate overnight or for at least 4 hours.

When ready to prepare the curry, place the butter in a small bowl and microwave to melt; this usually takes a minute.

When melted there will be a fatty white residue on the bottom of the bowl, the whey, and a golden "clarified" butter on top. For this recipe you want to use the clarified butter and discard the white residue.

Take most of the clarified butter to brown one large onion (cut in half and then thinly sliced). Once brown, add the meat in parts to the pan. Pour 1 cup of water into the now empty marinade dish to capture all of the spices from the mixture. Pour this into the meat. Add the tomato paste. Cover and let simmer for 1 hour. Stir and let simmer for 30 minutes more. Add a bit of cream. Chop coriander/cilantro bunch. Add to the curry along with the tomato. Let simmer uncovered for 30 minutes. The curry is ready when it has reached the desired consistency. I let the liquid evaporate until I am left with a very velvety curry sauce. Serve with mango chutney and basmati rice.

Extra condiments—shredded toasted coconut, chopped hard-boiled eggs, crushed peanuts. To my memory, the toppings are what made Pop-pop's curry so special.

Powelton Avenue

Not far from Reno Street, in another part of West Philadelphia, my parents and I lived in the top-floor apartment of my maternal grandparents' house, a large red brick Victorian row house that today accommodates three apartments and a basement flat. Then, it was all for us; "us" being my mother's parents, my mother's youngest brother [who was like a brother to me due to our being so close in age], me, my mother, and my father.

Josephine, my grandmother, was a great cook of southern staples like fried chicken and biscuits, and New England staples of meat, two vegetables, and mashed potatoes. Grandma Jo was also known as the teenage grandma because of her love of connecting with the young people; she was a "glamma" before its time.

The front of the house, going from the street to the house, began with a wrought-iron waist-high gate with a latched door that swung open. This door opened onto a shiny stone path that took you to the wooden steps to the house. On either side of the path were a few square meters of grassy area. The stairs led up to the porch and the front door. Most people stopped at the porch because that is where the house really began. It was a gathering spot for neighbors, friends, and relatives; most of the time, you did not need to go any farther because someone was usually sitting there, ready to converse. Big Ed, mother's father, was the main inhabitant or, as he would say, "porch monkey," seated with his slender legs crossed, Chesterfield cigarette in hand and billboard-worthy smile to greet you, his sharp wit kept you in his company. He could break it down. The mailman always had a minute to stop for an update on what was happening in the neighborhood and, more importantly, on where the jobs were coming and going in the city. Sometimes. Sometimes we just watched the world and the cars go by. In many a quiet hour, before my parents came home from work, Big Ed and I sat on the porch swinging in silence as the blue trail of cigarette smoke funneled above his head.

In my mind, that porch was our living room most days of the year, at least those days when one could sit outside. There was a swinging, rocking sofa, chairs, tables, and the railing ledges to serve as extra seating when needed. The porch was made of wood painted the color of slate. It looked nice against the red brick of the house. The main seating area was around a large picture window that looked in on the sitting room. Big Ed sat there in his free time while grandmother came out from time to time to have a rest from tending to meals and the house to cackle, "How y'all doin?" or, "What you say?" to whoever was visiting.

I was what my mother called a "very settled" little person. Every Friday, on his way home from work, Pop-pop picked me up to spend the weekend at home with him and Nana on Reno Street. For my Friday weekend departure, I always wore a dress, with tone-coordinated ankle socks trimmed in lace, polished shoes, and a part like a tightrope down the middle of my scalp, with my hair finishing in two braids that were held in place by ribbons or ribbon-shaped plastic barrettes.

I sat at the top of the steps at a certain time every Friday to wait for Pop-pop's arrival. I did not play in the grass, I did not converse, I did not need company, and I did not fidget or run around. After all, mother had said not to get dirty. I did not move from my spot on the steps until he walked through the gate. For as long as we lived on Powelton Avenue and from the time I could walk and obey my mother, every Friday evening, I sat on the porch at the house waiting for Pop-pop to pick me up. I was his ritual.

I always saw Pop-pop parking his car right in front of the house.

"Ooo, Pop-pop got the same parking space again," Mother always said with a smile.

"I don't know how he does that." She had a bet going with herself that one day he would not get that space.

Coming through the gate with his small cloth fedora worn on his angle, as soon as he reached the stairs, Pop-pop gathered me in his arms.

"There's my girl."

We never left for Reno Street right away. Pop-pop enjoyed the porch too. Before leaving, he would sit, converse, and share his peanuts in the shell. Without fail, he came with a fresh, warm bag. They were a treat for me. Everyone on the porch just enjoyed each other and being together. As dusk turned to dark, fireflies started to appear, and empty peanut shells were in a pile, inevitably, the phone rang. It was Nana calling to ask what we were still doing "over there" when we knew dinner was ready. We were never ready to leave.

Pop-pop swallowed whatever peanut was left in his mouth, and exhaled before sighing his reply, "All right, Minerva. We're coming."

We said our goodbyes and went down to the car. Behind me I heard:

"Y'all take care."

"We'll see you Sunday night, Annette."

I rode in the back seat. I was off to Pop-pop and Nana's house until Sunday dinner when my parents came to collect me and visit with Pop-pop and Nana before heading back to Powelton Avenue to begin a new week.

Life was sweet.

My parents and I soon left behind the rhythms of grandparents, aunties, uncles, and cousins of Philly, Reno Street and Powelton Avenue, to continue my parents' life, moving around the country as a military family.

My mother carried on our West Philly taste for culinary exploration by always "experimenting" with non-American cuisine. As we moved around the country, from south to north and from east coast to west, with my father's postings often taking him overseas while we remained in the United States, savory French crepes stuffed with chicken and mushrooms, steamed Chinese pork buns, wok-fried dishes, stollen, elaborate gingerbread houses at Christmas, and stone-baked pizza were some of her hallmarks. But it is the most traditional dishes I associate with home in America that I still make to this day. Of course, now, often with a twist.

Recipes from Home

Salads—Starters—Soups

MACARONI SALAD

A summertime favorite. Everyone loved my mother's tuna macaroni salad.

Start to finish: 30–40 minutes
Serves 4

2 jars drained tuna fish packed in water
One diced hard-boiled egg

½ cup diced green pepper
¼ cup diced yellow onion
¼ cup diced celery
¼ cup diced dill pickle or gherkin

Generous teaspoon Dijon mustard
4 cups cooked elbow macaroni
2 tablespoons apple cider vinegar

Mayonnaise to suit taste, at least 4 tablespoons

Keep the cooked pasta shells at room temperature. Mix all of the ingredients except the mayonnaise in a large bowl. Add the mayonnaise last.

Serve on sliced, lightly salted beefsteak tomatoes.

FISH SOUP

Reminiscent of New England chowders, but without shellfish due to my mother's shellfish allergies. Having a naval officer father and spending a few years in New England, chowders were a staple.

Start to finish: 90 minutes
Serves 4–6

500–600 grams halibut steak (2 steaks)
or cod, or other firm white fish

1 large celery stalk
½ large white or yellow onion
1 cup curly parsley
1 garlic clove
1 small lemon
1 small shallot
1 medium carrot
1 small tomato, deseeded
2 thyme branches
1 bay leaf
3 small potatoes, skinned and cut into large cubes

1 chicken bouillon cube
1 cup water
Black and white pepper

2 tablespoons butter
1 cup skimmed milk
Heaping tablespoon crème fraîche or ¼ cup single cream

Melt the butter in a large saucepan on medium heat. Add the thyme and bay leaf to the butter. While simmering, chop all the vegetables and then add all but the potatoes to the pan.

Slightly increase heat. Rinse fish steaks and add skin-side down to the pan. Push the vegetables around to make room for the fish. Season liberally with salt and black pepper. Cook for 7 to 10 minutes, stirring after 5 minutes. Increase heat to low-high and add the juice of one lemon. Make sure lemon pips do not go into the saucepan. Stir this around and let cook for another 10 minutes on medium heat.

Add the potatoes. Add the milk, water, and crushed bouillion cube, stir, and bring to a light boil. Cover and reduce heat to simmer. Let simmer for up to 90 minutes.

Remove the bones from the steaks and add cream, salt, and white pepper to taste.

CHOPPED SALAD
Start to finish: 1 hour
Serves 4

2 hard-boiled eggs, chopped
2 cups diced smoked ham/turkey
(or mix of both)

2 Bibb or romaine lettuces, quartered and chopped
1 small fennel bulb, thinly sliced
1 large carrot, parboiled and diced
2 radishes, thinly sliced
1 garlic clove, crushed
½ cup green olives, diced
1 cup diced red peppers
½ cup long shallot, diced
Dozen or so cherry tomatoes, halved
2 cups steamed and chopped string beans
½ cup chopped green pepper
½ cup chopped sweet white onion

Mustard
Apple cider vinegar
Salt
Fresh ground pepper

1 cup diced sheep cheese like Ossau-Iraty
Olive oil

Mix all of the vegetables together in a large bowl. In a small bowl, whisk 1 tablespoon of mustard with 2 tablespoons of vinegar. Add salt and fresh ground pepper. Whisk in about ½ cup of olive oil to create an emulsion. Toss the salad with the chopped eggs and emulsion. You can also dress this with a light, ready-made Caesar dressing.

TOMATO SOUP

I don't know how much tomato soup I consumed as a child, but it was such a staple growing up that I had to learn how to make a close version when I moved out of the United States. Tomato soup and grilled cheese sandwiches were a lunchtime favorite.

Start to finish: 120 minutes
Serves 6

A dozen or so plum tomatoes
Sprigs fresh rosemary *(optional)*
1 large leek
1 large potato *(optional)*

Fresh ground black pepper
3 cups chicken stock, vegetable stock, or water
Tomato paste *(optional)*
Celery salt *(optional)*

Olive Oil
Crème fraîche *(optional)*

A variety of tomatoes will make an excellent soup. Wash and stem the tomatoes. Set the oven to 200°C/400°F.

Cut the tomatoes in half and remove all of the seeds, keeping as much of the flesh as possible. Place the tomatoes in a roasting pan. You can season the tomatoes with olive oil, salt, and fresh ground pepper if desired, as well as some sprigs of fresh rosemary.

Clean and chop up the leek and add to the roasting pan with the tomatoes. Roast the tomatoes for about an hour or until the skin begins to bubble and char. Sometimes a bit of water may need to be added to the pan to prevent the juices from burning. Once done, remove the pan from the oven and begin to pull the skin away from the tomatoes. This may be done imperfectly, but the skin should be easy to remove. I discard the skin. You can also rub the oil and residue of the skin onto thin slices of bread that can then be used for croutons.

Pour the roasted tomato and leek into a saucepan. There should be 750 ml to 1 liter of roasted tomato. Add your stock of choice and, optionally, one diced potato. If desired, season with a dash of celery salt, and a tablespoon or so of tomato paste. Cook for about 20 minutes and then blend with a hand blender.

The stock can be adjusted to suit the desired thickness of the soup. If a cold season, add a dollop of crème fraîche to the soup. If served in warm weather, serve au naturel.

The soup can be garnished with parsley-coated croutons.

GRANDMA'S CORN CHOWDER
Start to finish: 2.5 hours
Main for 6

6 large knockwurst sausages
(chicken, turkey, or pork),
sliced bottle-cap thickness

2 chopped celery stalks
1 large leek, chopped
1 bunch parsley, chopped
1 8-ounce can corn or 4 ears' worth, husked
1 potato, cut into small cubes

1 can creamed corn
1 8-ounce/400g can chopped tomatoes
2 cups chicken stock
Fresh ground pepper

1 cup light cream
Butter

Brown the knockwurst in 25g/1 tablespoon of butter. Add the leek, celery, and parsley, and sauté for 5 minutes. Add fresh ground pepper, corn, tomatoes, and stock. Bring to a boil and quickly reduce the heat. Add the potatoes. Simmer for 2 hours. Add 1 cup of cream. Heat through. Salt to taste.

VEGETABLE SOUP

Like tomato soup, vegetable beef soup was a staple. More vegetable than meat, the meat is now optional.

Chopping time: 20 minutes; 90 minutes to 3 hours cooking time
Serves 6

1 slice oxtail or marrow bone *(optional)*

16 oz or 4 cups chopped tomato
1 celery stalk, diced
1 zucchini, diced
1 small turnip, peeled and diced
1 large potato, peeled and diced
1 large carrot, diced
2 cups string beans, diced
2 cups fresh garden peas
Kernels of 4 ears of fresh corn
2 cups of curly parsley, chopped
1 large leek, diced

Bay leaf
Bouillon cube
2 tablespoons tomato paste
1 large tablespoon flour

Olive Oil

Some people like their vegetable soup chunky, and others finely diced. I aim to have all of the vegetables pea-size.

To add depth to the flavor of the soup, I recommend roasting the vegetables on high heat for an hour with the bone/tail if using. If using the tail, do add a cup or two of water to the roasting pan. You can season with a splash of olive oil if desired, salt, pepper, and the other seasonings as preferred.

Once roasted, transfer to a deep stockpot, add ½ liter of water or stock, and simmer until the meat comes off the bone.

Then, while briskly whisking, slowly pour about 1½ cups of cold water into the flour. Stir into the soup mix along with the tomato paste. Add salt as desired and 1 bouillon cube.

Let simmer for half an hour. If making the soup meatless, simmer for an hour before adding the flour and paste.

For me, a hearty oxtail soup is the "American version" of chili. Dad's work took us west to California for a good part of my childhood. Growing up on the West Coast in the 1960s and early 1970s, you could still meet men who had been real gauchos, or cowboys and ranch hands, in their boyhood in the American West. One of my fondest memories is of a cowboy friend of my parents taking over the kitchen to make oxtail soup. If you can't get oxtail, use veal or lamb in the following Osso Soup recipe.

OSSO SOUP
Start to finish: 5 hours
Serves 6–8

1 slice veal shank (osso bucco) or
1 slice lamb shoulder with the bone in

One whole yellow onion
8–10 peppercorns
Bay leaf
White parts of 1 leek, chopped
1 diced carrot
3 cups fresh chopped spinach
1 large potato, chopped
1 cup fresh peas
1 cup chopped, raw string beans
A few celery leaves, chopped

1 vegetable bouillon cube
Flour

Simmer the meat in just enough water to cover the meat along with the yellow onion, bay leaf, and peppercorns for approximately 3 hours, until it falls off the bone. Remove the bay leaf, the meat, and bone from the broth and set aside.

Hold a handheld blender over the onion and blend with the broth only. Do not blend the meat.

Season the broth with fine sea salt to taste.

Add the vegetables except for the peas and let cook until desired tenderness. (I prefer 1 hour of slow cooking). Whisk 1 tablespoon of flour with not more than 1 cup of cold water.

Stir the flour mixture into the soup. Salt to taste. Let cook for at least twenty minutes.

Add the fresh peas and cook for 20 more minutes. Pull meat apart into bite-sized pieces and, if desired, remove marrow from bones and stir into the soup.

Serve as a main course.

Oxtail variation: Do not add spinach or peas, but do add pinto beans. Also, replace the leek with a whole large yellow onion, peeled, of course.

SALMON CROQUETTES

Start to finish: 30–40 minutes
Serves 4

418g/14 oz cooked salmon
2 eggs

½ green pepper, finely diced
½ small onion, grated
¼–½ cup mashed potatoes *(optional)*

Fine breadcrumbs

Evaporated milk *(optional)*
Oil for frying

Canned salmon can be used for this recipe. Place the salmon in a large mixing bowl and flake it with a fork. Add the green pepper and onion, season with salt and fresh ground pepper to taste, and mix well. If desired, the mashed potato can also be mixed in with the salmon. Add a drizzle of evaporated milk if desired. The mix should be heavy and easy to handle in hand to form the cakes. Place in the refrigerator to chill for ten minutes.

Place the breadcrumbs in a bowl. Beat two eggs in a separate bowl. Add the chilled water to the eggs to thin them out a bit. Heat ½ inch of oil in a nonstick frying pan.

Remove the salmon from the fridge. You can make 4 to 6 croquettes of medium size or 8 small croquettes. I prefer the croquettes flat and disc-shaped, like hamburgers. Dip each croquette in the egg and then coat well with breadcrumbs. Set on a plate. When done coating, fry in the oil. Each side should brown. The color may also depend on the type of breadcrumbs used. The fish is already cooked, so you are looking for a nice crust. When done, drain on paper towel and serve. Mother served her croquettes with asparagus and buttered boiled potatoes covered with chopped curly parsley. They also go well with steamed string beans.

Entrées

FRIED CHICKEN
Start to finish, excluding overnight brining: 40 minutes.

Fried chicken is my ultimate comfort food. In the kitchen, however, it used to be one of the things I least enjoyed preparing. Flour can go everywhere despite the best efforts at containment; a tough bird can make the end result less satisfying. Everyone thinks there is a secret to frying chicken. Once, a friend, upon tasting my fried chicken, asked me if I had made it "using [my] grandmother's recipe." Josephine, my maternal grandmother, fried the most perfect chicken in an iron skillet and baked meltingly delicious biscuits to go with them. That particular evening with my friend, I had not used my grandmother's seasoning, but it still came out near perfect and comment-worthy, I believe, thanks to her trusted rules which I now hold as sacred.

You need the three "B"s—at least—to obtain a superior fried chicken. They are:

Brining
Buttermilk
Brown paper bag

Brining:
Brining consists of soaking the chicken pieces in seasoned salt water overnight so the flesh absorbs the flavor; this allows for added moisture and the breakdown of some of the tough muscles. Take a medium to small chicken and cut into eight pieces. Remove pinfeathers (you can burn the stubborn ones off) and clean the chicken with the juice of one lemon; I then

rinse with water. Liberally pierce the chicken pieces with a sharp knife. Set aside while you prepare the brine.

Flavor is key to brining. Brine for one chicken:

Dissolve 1 tablespoon of salt in 2 cups of hot water. Add a few peppercorns and one crushed bay leaf to the salt water. Pour into a large bowl and add 3 liters of cold water to the mixture. Add thin slices of half a yellow onion. Place the chicken pieces in the brine. Cover and place in the refrigerator overnight and/ or until ready to cook (4 to 6 hours is a minimum).

Buttermilk:
When you are ready to fry the chicken, you first make the buttermilk if you do not have any store-bought. I never buy buttermilk; I always make it. Making buttermilk is easy. You add one tablespoon of apple cider vinegar to a measuring cup. Top the cup up with whole milk to the 1-cup mark. Stir it and let rest to thicken for ten minutes or so. Prepare the flour to coat the chicken. For one chicken you will need about 4 cups of flour. Season the flour with 1 teaspoon each of paprika, ground black pepper, salt, and garlic powder.

Brown bag:
I believe this is the real key to frying chicken. Somehow the flour coating adheres best to the chicken when applied in a brown paper bag. Place the seasoned flour into a large brown paper bag. Grocery store brown bags are fine. I place the brown bag in a plastic grocery bag so that the flour does not fly out of the seams of the bag during the vigorous shaking.

A brown bag can be hard to find in Europe, where I now live. I have a whole collection of brown bags accumulated from various bakers and shops, all in waiting to be used to shake my chicken in their coating.

Pat the chicken pieces dry with paper towel. Place the chicken pieces in the buttermilk. Coat it well with the milk. Then place the chicken pieces one at a time in the brown bag with the flour so that each piece is resting on flour, not on other chicken pieces. Roll the opening of the bag shut and then shake the bag to coat the chicken. Shake well, left to right, upside down. Let settle and then gingerly open the bag so you are not hit with a flour cloud on opening. Remove each piece of chicken and place on a nonstick baking tray or wax paper.

Preheat oven to 160°C/325°F.
Now inspect the coating of the chicken. If flesh shows or you find some areas of coating sparse, dip the piece of chicken quickly back into the buttermilk and then quickly into the flour bag for another shake. Remove to set. Let the flour set on the chicken for at least 5 minutes.

Heating the oil.
Take a large heavy skillet. Pour the oil in until it is about an inch deep, unless of course you have a deep fryer. I prefer to fry with peanut oil, safflower oil, or tallow. Neither peanut oil or tallow burns or gets too smoky at high temperatures. In the past, I have also used Crisco or even a combination of Crisco and peanut oil. Use any vegetable oil on hand, other than olive oil, if you do not have peanut oil. Season the oil with salt and start heating the oil at a low temperature.

Turn the heat on the oil to medium-high when ready to fry. Place chicken pieces in the hot oil to fry. The pieces should not touch. Fry until desired crispiness and color. Turn over; season the face-up side with a bit of salt. Once done, place on a nonstick baking pan. Bake in the oven for 20 minutes. This ensures the meat is cooked to the bone.

Enjoy.

FAST FRIED CHICKEN

When a reliably tender chicken is available, a craving is strong, and there is no time to brine, I simply fry.

Start to finish: 65 minutes
Serves 4

Season 8 clean chicken pieces with an herb season-all, such as Ma Bell's, salt, pepper, and garlic powder—take an equal measure of each and a half measure of the pepper. You can let the seasoning penetrate the chicken for 20 minutes. Dip and cover in self-rising flour and then dip in the full-fat milk or buttermilk (to make, see buttermilk in previous Fried Chicken recipe). Then coat with flour again. This can be repeated if desired; the more coatings you build up, the crunchier the finish. Let the coated chicken rest for 5 to 10 minutes before frying.

Heat an inch of cooking oil on medium in a large skillet. Season the oil with a bit of salt. When good and hot, fry the chicken pieces. You want all sides to be golden brown. You will have to turn the chicken during the frying to get all of the sides. After frying, remove the chicken from the oil, place on a cloth or paper towel and then place in a baking dish to finish in an oven at 150°C/300°F for 25 minutes to cook through to the bone.

SAUSAGE AND PEPPERS

I had to take a bit of "local" Philly fare with me.

Use quality sausage links, or Italian pork sausages. Split length-wise and grill, pan fry, or broil as desired.

Heat any leftover Rainbow Peppers (next page) in a shallow pan. Add the cooked sausages to the peppers and let simmer for ten minutes or so. Serve on a baguette or with spaghetti.

RAINBOW PEPPERS

Start to finish: 60 minutes
Serves 4–6

1 red, 1 yellow, and 1 orange bell pepper
1 fennel bulb
1 zucchini
Juice of 1 lemon
Olive oil

Thinly slice all of the vegetables. Toss in a baking dish with the fennel, olive oil, and lemon juice. Let roast at 220°C/425°F for 20 minutes and then at a low temperature (170°C/350°F) for another 30 minutes.

SWEDISH MEATBALLS

Making these reminds me of the wonderful taste adventures my mother took us on as children with her family meals and party buffets. It brings me a moment of peace.

Start to finish: 75 minutes
Serves 6–8

½ pound ground veal
½ pound extra-lean beef

2 chopped onions
½ cup chopped parsley
1 bay leaf

Allspice or nutmeg
Juniper berries
Garlic powder
½ cup beef stock
Cognac or sherry to taste
White pepper
Flour
1 thick slice country white bread
without the crusts

¼ cup heavy cream
2 tablespoons crème fraîche
Milk
5 tablespoons butter

Place bread in a bowl and soak it with milk. Season with salt, pepper, 2 pinches of allspice (or grated nutmeg and juniper berry), and 1 teaspoon of garlic powder.

With a fork, completely mash the bread and spices, and add the meat. Season again with salt, pepper, 2 pinches of allspice (or ground nutmeg and juniper berry), 1 teaspoon of garlic powder. Mix well.

Sauté onions with bay leaf in the butter. Salt as desired.

Form meatballs by hand rolling a heaping teaspoon per meatball and coat in flour.

Push the onions in the pan aside and add meatballs to the onion.

Brown the meatballs in batches if necessary.

With all of the meatballs in the pan, add the beef stock. Bring to a bubble, add the sherry or cognac if desired, reduce heat, cover, and simmer for 15 minutes.

Add the parsley and cream. Simmer uncovered for 15 minutes. The sauce will thicken.

Add the crème fraîche. Do not stir; let the crème fraîche melt and disperse over 10 minutes. Gently stir the sauce and meatballs. The sauce should be sufficient to nicely smother egg noodles.

MACARONI

This version of macaroni pasta is inspired by my boys' love of American mac and cheese and mine of the wonderful *macaronades* I would come to love in France. More than a pasta bake, a *macaronade* can be made with a well-rested, perhaps days' rested, beef stew thoroughly intertwined with soft macaroni shells and a white sauce, béchamel. The pasta is not al dente because it has absorbed the extra liquid from the stew. Heaven. This is enjoyed as a main dish. The possibilities are endless when one thinks of adding stewed meats or vegetables.

Start to finish: 1 hour 45 minutes
Serves 6

1 egg

2 garlic cloves, finely chopped

White pepper
Nutmeg
1 heaping tablespoon white flour
400g macaroni elbows, boil an extra 2–3 minutes

2 cups grated sharp white cheddar
125 to 150 g/8 tablespoons salted butter
1 cup grated extra-sharp orange or white cheddar
(A variety of cheeses can be used if cheddar is not available, so use any cheese you like such as Cantal, Ossau-Iraty, Emmental)
3–4 cups skim milk
1 tablespoon crème fraîche

In a skillet, melt the butter on low heat. Add the garlic and sauté, still on low heat, for about 5 minutes. Place the flour in a bowl and slowly whisk the milk in, then pour this mixture into the garlic and butter, increasing to a medium heat. Whisk and raise the temperature a bit until the mixture starts to thicken. Constant attention should be given to whisking so that the flour does not settle on the bottom of the pan. Allow the flour mixture to cook for about 7 minutes, then lower the heat. Season the sauce with salt and pepper to taste and nutmeg (not more than ¼ teaspoon). I do not oversalt the sauce, because the cheese is salty.

Add the cheeses and stir until they melt. Add the crème fraîche. Crack the entire egg into the cheese sauce and whisk in vigorously. Sometimes I only add the yolk. This is according to taste. My mother adds a good teaspoon of spicy mustard rather than egg to her cheese sauce. All work well.

Once all ingredients are in, let the sauce cook in the pan for a total of 20 minutes on low heat. Remove from the heat and stir in the cooked macaroni. I like to boil my pasta until very soft, so for a few extra minutes, as this allows for a softer, creamier finished dish after baking. Place the mixture into a baking dish and bake in the oven at 180°C/350°F for approximately 30 minutes or longer, depending on how brown you like the top crust.

Optional: A mixture of shredded cheese, chopped fresh parsley, and panko breadcrumbs can lightly coat the top of the casserole.

Desserts

ICE CREAM SUNDAES
Start to finish: 20 minutes

Not adept at baking, I never attempted making my grand-mother's gravity-defying cakes. I cannot do everything, so ice cream is my go-to dessert. In most places, one is sure to find ice cream easier than good baked goods. And ice cream still takes me back to the childhood joy of new and favorite flavors. Everyone loves customizing their ice cream or enjoying a parfait-like sundae.

Always use a quality vanilla ice cream. I don't use any other flavor of ice cream in a sundae. Any other flavors you may want, such as chocolate, coffee, or mint, you can achieve by having it as one of the toppings for that vanilla base.

Toppings:

Rather than buying fruit sauces, microwave fresh berries in an instant and then blend to create a natural, fruity sauce.

First, clean the desired fruits, such as blueberries or raspberries, and clean and slice strawberries before placing in microwave-safe dishes. Sixty to 90 seconds is sufficient to burst and heat the fruit, creating a juicy but fruity emulsion. Once it is removed from the microwave, you can further crush the fruit with a fork or blend. You can also place the cooked fruit in a sieve so you do not have the seeds in the sauce. Pinches of lemon zest and sugar can be added as desired, but ripe fruit in season usually won't need anything to bring out its flavor.

For crunch, add crushed nuts such as walnut, almond, macadamia, and pistachio.

For chocolate sauce, simply melt squares of chocolate on a low heat or in a bain-marie and whisk with very little water to achieve desired consistency. Chocolate can be lumpy when melting, so slowly add water while whisking until the chocolate begins to smooth out. The type of chocolate used will determine how the sauce liquefies. For mint-flavored chocolate, infuse some fresh mint leaves in hot water for 5 minutes. Use this water to whisk into the chocolate.

Ripe bananas, grilled or stewed sliced peaches, and cherries are also classic toppings. Cherries can be ripe and fresh or in a liqueur.

Variation: STRAWBERRY ICE CREAM
Coarsely chop 2 cups of ripe strawberries and mix in with a pint of soft vanilla bean ice cream. Leave to chill. Toast ½ cup of almond slivers to sprinkle on ice cream when ready to serve.

APPLE AND BERRY ALMOND CRUMBLE

If you can't make a cake, make a crumble. If you have fruits you don't want to go to waste, make a crumble.

Start to finish: 60 minutes
Serves 6

  1 red apple, but any variety will do, peeled and cored
  Salt
  1½ cups raspberries
  1½ cups blueberries
  1½ cups blackberries
  Lemon juice

Slice the apple with a mandoline.
Layer on the bottom of a round quiche dish.
Sprinkle with a pinch of salt and a tablespoon of lemon juice
Mix the berries and place on top of the apple.

Prepare the crumble topping by working together:
⅔ tablespoon brown sugar
½ stick salted butter
1 heaping tablespoon white flour
1¾ cups sliced almonds

Place the crumble mixture over the fruit.

Bake at 190°C/375°F for 30 minutes.

Serve with vanilla ice cream

Variation: Mango and peaches, and apple. In both cases you want 5 cups of fruit.

Leaving Home

I left home for university at eighteen. I never returned to live, although I always had a key to my parents' home. On leaving home to make our way in the world, they told each of us siblings, "There is always a room for you at the inn." During my university years, I went to Washington, D.C. to study international affairs. After my second year, I had the opportunity to participate in a work-study program abroad focusing on migration and refugee issues. I was eventually placed with an international organization in Nairobi, Kenya, for six months. My time living in Kenya solidified my decidedly adventurous palate as I tried stews, grilled meats that were unusual to me, more curries, and wonderfully spiced coffees. During my first two-plus decades of life, well, food was part of the adventure of life. I never joined in for the staid, Western hotel food.

In Nairobi, I loved the curry houses with communal tables for the mostly male office workers and the home-run restaurants in the refugee quarters where the actual dishes were communal. The taste of stewed goat or chicken in spicy sauces, grilled corn, and injera are still fresh on my tongue. I wish I had cooked then, to have a recipe to remember.

Being food-adventurous does come with risks. One afternoon, following a nap, I woke up, opened my eyes, and was unable to see for a few hours. This was presumably an unexplained reaction to eating rancid butter. Cautionary tale. By the end of my studies, I had tried almost everything, culinary-wise, put before me. In all my years of youthful tasting adventures, I never thought that I would turn my hand to serious cooking.

University in Washington, D.C., was followed by three years of law school in New York City. After obtaining my law degree, I returned to Washington, D.C., Capitol Hill–bound with dreams of becoming a specialist on a committee and eventually the first Black female senator in the US Senate. That history was to be made by others.

Returning to Washington after three years in New York, I found many of my university friends still there, having decided to settle in D.C. Although now a lawyer, "counsel," on the Hill, I returned somewhat to my former student life with the group vibes of the 1980s like nights at jazz supper clubs and dinner parties with friends. I met my first husband (actually, the only) at one such party given by university friends of mine who were also friends of his. He was on sabbatical from his firm in Paris, France, to work in an international development organization. The evening was marked by feisty discussions and the host's feast of wonderful dishes from Senegal. It was over a plate of a savory rice dish, and heated political banter, that I took note of my future husband. Unbeknownst to me, it was the beginning of a journey that would take me far from Capitol Hill. That was early 1990.

After months of bumping into each other at parties and gatherings, hanging out a bit ourselves with friends, and becoming the confidante of a woman who had a crush on him, by April I kind of realized that I did, too. My birthday came, and I decided I needed to be a woman of emotional courage. I rang my future husband to share my feelings. They were mutual. A very low-key courtship and coupling, meeting family members, sharing dreams about how we would do things differently—how we would command our ships—progressed to engagement by the end of the year, a wedding in 1991, and a future outside the United States.

Part 2

EUROPE

TRAVELS IN "SIBERIA"

Six short weeks after marrying and two years out of grad school, I became a trailing spouse, moving overseas to Paris, France, without a job or, I soon discovered, the language proficiency to jump right into local life. Granted, many an American lives in a foreign country without ever learning to speak the language, but, oh, what they are missing. At the time of my marriage, some of my extended family of aunts, uncles, and family friends discussed, bemoaned, and fretted over my move to Paris. It seemed as if I was moving to Siberia. I pushed back on that and embraced the experience.

As a jobless newlywed in France, time was on my side to learn to cook. In an old-fashioned sort of way, marriage brought me around to tackling and developing culinary skills. Alongside a year of intensive language lessons, I focused on food (test-tasting every *pain au chocolat* from the many patisseries I explored was an early obsession) and new-to-me ways of preparing it. I found an unexpected food passion: from the other side of the table, the kitchen and the supply side. Eating, which I had now enjoyed for close to three decades, took on a richer meaning when learning to prepare what would go on the table. I relished the challenge of a new learning curve by preparing dishes such as eggplant-stuffed rolled lamb shoulder, quail stuffed with veal, and on.

Enduring lessons about preparing food from those early days in Paris still guide me.

For our first "couples' night," I had to prepare a Saturday night dinner at home for friends. The wife was American, and the husband was French. One arrived at our lovely duplex flat after climbing four flights of stairs. The kitchen was again up another flight of stairs, tucked away in a corner and open onto the living and dining area. On reaching the top floor, not too breathlessly, the French husband saw how neat it was and, after saying hello, of course, commented, "Mmm, well, they say a clean kitchen is a sign of a good cook." Following the obligatory cheek-to-cheek, he told us how he anticipated having a good meal because of the presentable condition of the kitchen.

I smiled while pondering his comment. He did not elaborate, but I did think further. Did he mean, "Okay, you are organized about cooking, you are not a panic cooker, you are comfortable cooking, etc., because there is not a cacophony of pots and pans, ends of carrots, bits of vegetables, spilt sauces creating slip hazards, meat oils all over the place, and/or butter wrappings on the floor"?

I do not recall what I prepared, but there was good wine throughout and excellent cheese and salad, which was de rigueur. Following dinner, the husband shared with me the name of his most sacred cookbook, *La Varenne Pratique*— proof, I like to think, of his appreciation of my efforts and the meal. That cookbook became and remains my foundation, alongside the love and knowledge of food from home. Every cook should have their own encyclopedic source for food.

Some of my other staple takeaways from French cooking were that oil emulsions can be just as good as butter and cream, what to look for when buying fresh fish (always check the moisture and color under the gills), and elaborating on salads as meals with *salades composeés*. Leftover veal loin from the recipe for Friday-Night Veal is ideal for a next-day *salad composé*.

The other thing I discovered in France is that cooking, real cooking, is quite a physical, bloody activity, and is not for wimps. A good cookbook will expand on carcasses and food alchemy. A strong wrist and firm grip facilitate skillful cutting through bone and cartilage and tough root vegetables.

The transition from American grocery store prepackaged items to having a selection of cuts from the head to toe of livestock, and fruits and vegetables according to their season, was involved. I was resolved not to rely on the French ready-made meals of Picard, M&S, or the lovely traiteur selections, while I had the time to indulge my fascination with Paris's fresh produce markets, cheeses, pastries, and my local butcher. Providence dictated that the first two floors of our building were occupied by the butcher. One of the best in Paris, in my book, and kindest. When I first entered the shop, I was overwhelmed by the variety of cuts I came to know, recipe by recipe, question by question, over the years with the gentle guidance of the butcher and *La Varenne Pratique*.

I came to appreciate a French approach to everyday food— that simplicity often yields the best results. Likewise, the quality of ingredients is of paramount importance because, at the end of preparation, the real goal is to bring out the best quality of a particular food, its essence. I can still hear the butcher's instructions, insisting that after cooking I let the meat rest before carving or come to a certain temperature before cooking. It is so important and beneficial to try and buy meat that is fed on what nature intended it to be fed on. Educating the palate is also a part of the process of simplicity—knowing the actual taste of a food—as is thinking about seasonality wherever you are. Eating seasonally was exciting. The arrival of fruits and vegetables was and can be an occasion.

> *He who distinguishes the true savour of his food can never*
> *be a glutton; he who does not cannot be otherwise.*
> —*Henry Thoreau*

Salads—Starters—Soups

FRENCH STRING BEANS WITH GOOSE LIVER

One of my favorite lunches, which a friend would always throw together while we sat around her rustic wooden kitchen table chatting under the beams of her attic flat in Paris's 7th arrondissement, is warm string bean salad *à la Française*! It was always enjoyed with a red table wine, like Beaujolais nouveau, and a crusty baguette.

Start to finish: 30 minutes
Serves 2–4

Goose foie gras (*optional*)

400g/8 cups French string beans, cleaned and trimmed
Shallots or garlic cloves, finely chopped

Red wine vinegar
Salt

2 tablespoons olive oil

Boil the string beans for eight to ten minutes. Quickly drain. Heat the olive oil in a large skillet with room to toss the beans around. Lightly salt the oil and add the string beans and garlic or shallots. Toss about for approximately 10 minutes, until the desired firmness of the beans. Add a splash of vinegar. Remove from the heat and toss with at least a cup of cubed foie gras pieces. Serve with warm bread, a leafy green salad if desired, and red wine.

Variation

Sauté steamed string beans in 2 tablespoons of olive oil with 3 chopped garlic cloves and one chopped shallot. Finish off with a tablespoon of balsamic vinegar. When done, mix in some smoked duck breast. Serve with country bread and red wine. To garnish, a few slivers of sun-dried tomatoes.

MACEDONIAN SALAD

A discovery from my days in France, this salad is a brilliant substitute for American potato salad. It can be evenly molded for presentation purposes, served with cold cuts and lettuce for a quick lunch, on a bed of lettuce and sliced tomatoes, and used as a stuffing for tomatoes. Although time-consuming to make from scratch, it is well worth the effort as the ready-made jar variety does not compare. Chop the vegetables while listening to a favorite podcast or chatting with the family or friends about their day.

Start to finish: 1 hour + marinating time
Serves 8

1 cup large garden peas or 1 cup of *petit pois*
1 cup chopped string beans
1 cup diced carrots
1 cup diced potato
1/4 cup turnip, diced (*optional*)
If turnips are not in season, they can be omitted.
1½ cups of flageolet beans (265 g canned, drained).
(Flageolets are small, very soft, light green kidney-shaped beans and may not be readily available. If you cannot source flageolet beans, cannellini beans are a nice substitute, and the salad can be prepared without any beans).
All of the vegetables should be cut roughly about the same size as the beans.

Red wine vinegar
Apple cider vinegar
Dijon mustard

¾ cup olive oil
4 tablespoons mayonnaise

Cook all of the vegetables in the following order in a liter of boiling water that has been seasoned with salt and 2 table-spoons of red wine vinegar. Cooking in vinegar water gives the vegetables a nice, faint pickled flavor. The vinegar is optional. If you boil the vegetables without vinegar, you can keep the drained water as a vegetable stock for a soup or gravy base.

Boil in the following order to ensure all of the vegetables are evenly cooked. Boil the string beans and carrots for 15 min-utes, then add the potato and the turnips, if using. Cook for another 15 minutes or until the potato is tender and not fall-ing apart. How quickly a potato cooks or holds up depends on the variety. Choose a hard potato variety if possible.

The peas require about 5 minutes to cook, so add them to the pot 5 minutes before you judge the potato is done. If using ready-to-eat canned *petit pois*, do not boil them. They will be added when the vegetables are cooled down. Thoroughly drain the vegetables and let them cool down. While they are cooling down, prepare the dressing for the vegetables.

Dressing:
Whisk together 1 heaping teaspoon of Dijon (my preferred brand is Maille) mustard, season as desired with Herbamare and freshly ground pepper to taste, and 2 tablespoons of apple cider vinegar. Then slowly whisk in a steady stream of ½ to ¾ cups of olive oil. Continuously and vigorously whisking while pouring in the oil will give a thick, mayonnaise-like emulsion.

Place the vegetables and flageolets in a bowl and mix in the vinaigrette with a rubber spatula. Let marinate for a couple of hours if possible.

When ready to serve, mayonnaise can also be added—approx-imately 4 tablespoons to taste. If the mayonnaise clots, stir in a teaspoon or so of vinegar and/or olive oil to smooth out the dressing. Mayonnaise can also be whisked into the vinaigrette emulsion before mixing in with the vegetables.

There are basics to always have on hand to pull together a salad: olive oil, any other oil you like (be it truffle or nut oil), Herbamare, a Dijon mustard, a hand whisk, a small glass bowl, vinegars, and your favorite ready-made dressings.

When ready to serve, you can toss in pita chips, homemade croutons, seeds, and/or nuts as desired to just about any salad.

MUENSTER, CUMIN, AND PEAR SALAD

Nectarines, peaches, plums, cherries, figs, and pears! Seasonal arrivals always lit up my market trips in Paris. They still do. The use of fruit in savory dishes was something I really came to appreciate in France. A quick duck breast pan-fry with sliced apples, baked pears, or this pear salad highlight the multitude of possibilities.

Start to finish: 30 minutes
Serves 4

Muenster cheese

4 ripe pears
Mâche
1 white and red chicory
Halved and lightly toasted hazelnuts

White wine vinegar
Cumin seeds
Baguette (approx. 20 in.)

Olive oil
Unsalted butter

Peel and core the pears. Slice and sauté in unsalted butter. Once the pears start to brown, sprinkle in a teaspoon of cumin seeds and let sizzle for a few minutes with the pears and butter. Remove from the pan to let cool.

Slice the baguette lengthwise and top both sides with slices of Muenster cheese. Place on a baking pan, ready to go under the grill.

Toss the cleaned Mâche and roughly chopped chicory with the hazelnuts and pears. When ready to serve, add a splash of white wine vinegar and olive oil.

Turn on the oven's top grill. Once hot, place the baguette under the oven grill to melt the cheese. Remove from the oven and slice the cheese baguette in 5-inch portion sizes. Plate the salad, and top with the Muenster toast.

ENDIVE SALAD

Crisp endives are great for a salad to cool down during heatwaves.

1 Bibb lettuce
3 small endives
1 red pepper
Sun-dried tomatoes (preferably in olive oil), minced
Chives

Salt
Pepper

Olive oil
Crème fraîche

Separate and wash the lettuce leaves. I like to remove any hard white stem centers. Slice the endives diagonally (about ½ inch slices); discard the hard bit in the center with the end. Cut the red pepper in half, deseed, and thinly slice. Take a large salad bowl and season it with salt, pepper, and 2 tablespoons of olive oil. Add the lettuce, endives, red pepper and about 3 tablespoons of tomatoes to the salad bowl and toss.

Dressing: In a bowl, add some chopped chives to 2 tablespoons of crème raiche. Then whisk a mustard vinaigrette (about ½ cup from a bottle) into the crème fraîche. Dress the salad with this dressing.

SMOKED TROUT SALAD

This salad is my go-to for a welcome change from smoked salmon. Growing up, Pop-pop and I did a lot of trout fishing. It made the best breakfasts. I was eager to try the smoked fillets I found in France.

Start to finish: 20 minutes
Serves 4

4 fillets smoked trout

Radicchio or baby Bibb lettuce
2 endives
2 ripe Bosc pears

Fresh ground pepper

White cheddar or Cantal in ribbon-like flakes
Horseradish dressing

Clean the lettuce and set aside. Prepare the endives. Remove the hard end and core. Take a plastic knife and slice the endive on the round, as thinly as you like. Peel the pears, cut lengthwise down the center and cut ½-inch slices. In a large bowl, toss these three ingredients. Add a pinch of pepper if desired.

Take the trout and lightly rinse with cold water and pat dry. Loosely break the trout up with your fingers. It should not be too flaky; you want nice morsels. When ready to serve, toss the salad leaves with a creamy horseradish dressing. Arrange the salad on a serving plate and top it with the trout and shavings of cheese.

France provided a culinary education that was mirrored in every country I visited in Europe. Travel throughout Europe is resplendent with how the most is made of what is local. When in Rome, do as the Romans. This was not lightly said, because the Romans know how to do food. So, when in Rome, eat like the Romans!

My favorite time to visit is during truffle season. A friend took me to her favorite neighborhood restaurant for the truffles, but they were preceded by the most magnificent vegetable buffet I had ever seen. I was captivated. Each local seasonal vegetable had been prepared to bring out the natural flavor. The buttered tagliolini with shavings of the season's white truffles we devoured after enjoying the buffet were good too. Sublime. The following four recipes are inspired by trips throughout Italy.

STUFFED ZUCCHINI FLOWERS
Start to finish: 1 hour
Serves 4

Eggs

12 zucchini flowers
Fresh mint, minced leaves
1 cup grated cucumber, without seeds
2 grated garlic cloves
Pinch lemon zest

Self-rising flour
Salt and fresh ground pepper
Basil *(optional)*
Oregano *(optional)*
Thyme *(optional)*

1 cup Greek yogurt
1 cup grated sheep cheese
Olive oil
Sunflower oil

Carefully clean the flowers. Lay on a paper towel to dry.

This dish requires a stuffing and batter.

For the stuffing, in a small bowl, mix the cucumber and thick Greek yogurt. Season with a dash of salt, fresh ground pepper, and lemon zest. Mix in grated cheese as desired, ½ to 1 cup. Leave in the fridge to chill.

For the batter, take a large bowl. Take ¾ to 1 cup of flour and a pinch of salt. While continually whisking, slowly add up to a cup of cold still or fizzy water to the flour. You want a batter that coats a spoon, so not too thin. Whisk in one egg, and a bit more salt. Then add the diced mint, about 1 tablespoon, and the grated garlic. Beat well. You can also add other fresh herbs, such as basil, oregano, thyme. If you do, use a small teaspoon of each.

Get out the yogurt mix. This should be firm and thick from the cheese. Take a teaspoon and stuff the flower cavity with the yogurt mixture. After stuffing each flower, gently twist and or pinch the top of the flowers to close.

Heat the sunflower oil in a nonstick skillet. You want the oil about an inch deep. Lightly salt the oil 2 minutes before it is ready. Gently place all of the stuffed flowers in the batter. Make sure all sides are coated. This can be done in batches. Take the batter-coated flowers one at a time and place in the oil to fry. They should be golden brown on each side. Remove to a towel on a baking tray to soak up any excess oil. Serve immediately.

Variation: Of course, you can stuff the flowers with whatever you like. Most important is to have a tasty batter.

SPAGHETTI WITH RED PEPPER REDUCTION

The challenge with this recipe is peeling the skin off the red peppers. Once that is done, it is the simplest recipe. I serve this lovely, sweet reduction as a starter. A complementary main could be grilled fish.

Start to finish: 90 minutes
Serves 4

12 red bell peppers
5 garlic cloves

A dozen black peppercorns
Salt

4 tablespoons olive oil

Blanch the red peppers to remove the skin, or cut in half, deseed, and remove the white excess membrane and peel the pepper with a vegetable peeler. Once you have the peeled and deseeded peppers, thinly slice them as well as the garlic cloves. Crush the peppercorns with a mallet. Take a saucepan, pour in the olive oil, lightly salt the oil, and heat on medium. Place all of the red peppers in the oil and slightly char the red peppers in the oil, then stir in the remaining ingredients and, optionally, a bit more salt. Cover and leave to simmer on a low heat setting for about an hour. Serve over spaghetti. I prefer this sweet sauce without grated cheese.

MUSHROOM AND WALNUT LASAGNA

I experienced this dish on one of my travels through Rome. The mushrooms used were in season, and I think it is easiest to do the same wherever you are. Chestnut, Portobello, and forest or wild mushrooms can all mix nicely for this lasagna. Mushrooms such as Portobello are to be peeled at the cap; I also slice off the dark brown underside and remove the stem. You can freeze the stems and use them later in stock. Whatever mushrooms you have, it is important to clean them to remove grit that you do not want to chew in the finished dish. I keep a baby toothbrush in the kitchen for such delicate jobs. This is a light lasagna that works well as a starter, or on a buffet.

Start to finish: 1 hour 45 minutes
Serves up to 8

4 cups raw, thinly sliced, chopped mushrooms
1–2 cups shelled whole walnut halves
Fresh basil, thinly julienned
1 cup flat Italian parsley, finely chopped
1 cup shallots, finely chopped

White pepper
Nutmeg
Thin lasagna pasta sheets
White wine
Flour

Butter
8–10 cups white cheese sauce
Double cream
1 pint/3–4 cups whole milk
2 cups Italian cheese (Parmesan, Taleggio, soft Pecorino)

Heat a large skillet over low heat. Increase the skillet heat to medium and add the mushrooms to the skillet. Sauté until most of the water from the mushrooms evaporates. This should take about 10 minutes. Add 4 tablespoons of butter to the mushrooms to continue cooking them.

Add the parsley and shallots to the mushroom mix. Sauté until the shallots brown. Increase the heat, and after a minute, toss in a cup of white wine. Let evaporate. Season with white pepper, salt to taste, and a healthy pinch of nutmeg. Remove the skillet from the burner and set aside while you make the white cheese sauce.

You need about 1 liter of sauce. Heat 4 tablespoons of butter in a saucepan. When melted, whisk in 2 tablespoons of flour. Keep whisking for a few minutes to "cook" the flour. Slowly pour in 1 pint of whole milk while continually whisking. You do not want the flour to clump. Once the flour is smoothly blended, bring the milk to a boil and then reduce the heat to low. Season with salt, white pepper to taste, and a pinch of nutmeg. Add the Italian cheese. I like a mix of Parmesan and Taleggio or, if using one cheese, a simple soft Pecorino. Mix well, and add 2 cups of heavy cream. Let simmer for another ten minutes. Essentially, you want the flour to have cooked in the saucepan for 20 minutes.

Stir the mushroom, parsley, and shallots into the white cheese sauce; this should be thin. Finally, add a cup of fresh chopped basil. Simmer on low while you crush the walnuts.

In a plastic bag or tea towel, loosely crush the walnuts to have about 1½ to 2 cups of crushed walnut pieces, as desired. Add to the sauce. Stir in well. Simmer for a few minutes and then remove from the heat.

Boil 10 to 12 lasagna sheets. Take a 12 x 12-inch baking dish and line the bottom with lasagna sheets. Pour ⅓ of the mushroom sauce over the lasagna sheets. Top with another layer of lasagna sheets. Pour ⅓ of the sauce over this second layer. Take the remaining sheets and place them on top of the sauce. You may not have enough sheets to completely cover the dish. That is fine. Pour the remaining sauce over the lasagna sheets. You can garnish with a bit of grated Parmesan cheese if desired. Bake at 175°C/350°F until bubbly, approximately 20 to 30 minutes.

The presentation of what is seasonal and local when traveling through Italy is unrivaled. The vegetable buffets, game, bread soups, truffles, pasta, and everyday cooking are overwhelming with the flavor of nature. Meat sauce is many a parent's staple and a dish, like tiramisu, I have tasted on many a trip there.

BOLOGNESE SAUCE

Making a good Bolognese sauce for me is as challenging as making the perfect omelet or scrambled eggs. All are often eaten and all look easy to make, but they are not. I have tried authentic recipes from Bologna, Italy, to recipes on the back of a jar of spaghetti sauce. My North Star for Bolognese was from a nondescript roadside family restaurant where we stopped on a drive from Pisa to Genoa to make our way back to Nice. The sauce was mixed in with the spaghetti. There was a tantalizing hint of salt when it hit your lips, and then the herbs and meat dominated the pasta. Memorable and delicious. Many years of trial and error (too watery, too bland, too complicated) have, however, yielded what appears to be a winning home recipe based on simplicity, taste, and texture. This Bolognese sauce tastes better the next day.

Start to finish: 2 hours
Serves 4–6

500g extra-lean, grass-fed ground beef

10 fresh button mushrooms
1 small carrot
2 garlic cloves
1 large onion
1 tablespoon oregano

Caramelized onion powder or cube
2 teaspoons good red wine
1 can (or 8 fresh) chopped tomatoes

⅓ cup heavy cream

Clean, stem, and mince the mushroom tops. Place in a pan on medium heat and sauté the mushrooms to remove the water.

While the mushrooms are cooking finely chop the garlic and add to the mushrooms. Let the garlic brown but not burn. Very finely dice the carrot and onion and stir into the garlic and mushrooms. Add 3 tablespoons (or more if you like) of olive oil to the vegetables. Season with salt (about 2 teaspoons), pepper, and the oregano. Sauté for 7 minutes and then add the onion cube and the water. Stir, cover, and let simmer for 15 minutes. Then stir in the ground beef. Then the wine, chopped tomatoes, and cream. Stir well and bring to a nice bubble. Cover, reduce the heat and let simmer for 45 minutes. Serve over cooked, buttered spaghettini.

While on university work study in Kenya years ago, I took a sleeper train to Mombasa during some of my leisure time. The train was well known for its traditional dining car, its tables with crisp linens and white glove service. The splendor was surpassed by the asparagus soup served at the start of the evening meal. I found that aroma and velvet smoothness again in Paris in French potages. A potage reflects the seasons and coats the spoon and the senses. I was thrilled to learn to make soup. My basic foundation for soup consists of leeks, potatoes, chicken stock, fresh ground pepper, and half a liter of water. Chicken stock can be replaced with mushroom or vegetable stock. Vegetables are full of salt and enough water to allow for dry sautéing and browning with no oils or fat. As an option, butter can be used for added flavor and the initial browning.

POTATO AND LEEK SOUP

Start to finish: 30 minutes
Serves 4

2 large baking potatoes, peeled
2 leeks, cleaned

Chicken or Vegetable bouillon

Olive oil
Butter *(optional)*

Coarsely cut the potatoes into chunks. Heat a splash of olive oil in a saucepan over medium. Add the leeks and 4 tablespoons of butter, if using. Salt and pepper. Let brown. Add the potatoes. Sauté for 2 or 3 minutes. Add ½ liter bouillon. Bring to a mild boil, cover, and cook until the potatoes are very soft.

Mix with a hand blender. Salt to taste. Adjust the bouillon depending on desired thickness of soup.

ASPARAGUS SOUP

This soup transports me right back to my first travel in the 1980s to the African continent and the dining car of the overnight train from Nairobi to Mombasa.

Start to finish: 60 minutes
Serves 6–8

24 green asparagus
1 large potato
1 leek, cleaned and chopped
1 celery stalk, chopped
1 tablespoon tarragon leaves, finely chopped
2 slices bread, finely cubed

White pepper

Olive oil
Crème fraîche *(optional)*

Turn the oven on to 200°C/400°F. Peel the potato and place in a baking pan. Drizzle with olive oil and season with salt and white pepper. Clean the asparagus and remove the hard ends. Peel the hard stalk with a vegetable peeler. Add the asparagus to the baking pan, along with the leek and celery. Toss the vegetables in the pan and roast for 20 minutes.

Remove from the oven and place the vegetables in a deep saucepan. Place on medium heat, then add the water. Bring to a boil and reduce to a simmer. While simmering, prepare croutons.

Roll the bread flat with a rolling pin. Cut into small crouton squares. Place the bread in the same baking pan used for the vegetables. Toss with the finely chopped tarragon. Bake in the oven until toasted. This will take about ten minutes.

Take a hand blender and blend the vegetables in the saucepan. A heaping tablespoon of crème fraîche can be added. Stir until melted. Serve the soup and garnish with croutons.

SPINACH SOUP
Start to finish: 70 minutes
Serves 6–8

1 small leek
400g or more of organic fresh spinach
1 small carrot

1 chicken bouillon cube
Fresh ground pepper

¼ cup heavy cream *(optional)*

Chop the leek and carrot and place in a pan on medium heat.

Clean the spinach and add to the leek and carrot. You may have to add the spinach in batches so that it fits in the pan. Let each batch cook down a bit.

Season with fresh ground pepper and the bouillon cube.

Add ½ liter of water to the vegetables, bring to a boil, and then reduce heat and let simmer for as long as you like, a minimum of 1 hour.

When ready to serve, blend the soup with a hand mixer right in the pot. Add about 3 pinches of salt and the cream and stir. Let simmer for 5 more minutes if you have added cream.

MUSHROOM SOUP

Start to finish: 90 minutes
Serves 4–6

8 cups uncooked chestnut mushrooms, chopped
1 leek
1 large white potato
Chervil for garnish
Shiitake or portobello mushrooms, a few for depth of flavor
½ to ¾ liter of vegetable or chicken stock

I do think it is worth investing in a mushroom brush that delicately cleans the mushroom. A practical alternative is a supersoft baby toothbrush. Keep it with the kitchen utensils.

Chop the ingredients and place all, except the chervil or any garnish, in a roasting pan. Oven roast at 200°C/400°F for about an hour. Place in a saucepan and blend with the stock. Heat through for half an hour or so and serve. Add garnish as desired.

EASY EGGPLANT BAKE
Start to finish: 90 minutes
Serves 6–8

1 large eggplant
Garlic
6 plum/Capri tomatoes
¼ cup fresh oregano
2 cups chopped fresh basil

Salt
Red wine vinegar

Olive oil
Parmesan cheese, grated *(optional)*

Thinly slice one large eggplant (½-inch thick), salt each side, and leave to sit for 15 to 20 minutes in a colander. The salt will sweat out the bitter juices. Thoroughly rinse the salt off the eggplant.

Coat the bottom of a round pie dish with one tablespoon of olive oil. Sprinkle chopped garlic clove as desired on the bottom.

Layer the eggplant in the pie dish.

Liberally sprinkle with chopped basil.

Roughly slice 6 or more plum/Capri tomatoes.

Layer the tomatoes on top of the herbs.

Sprinkle with oregano.

Mix olive oil and red wine vinegar to create half a cup of an emulsion. Take a half-cup measure and add 3 tablespoons of vinegar. Top up with olive oil. Then blend the two to make vinaigrette. Pour over the tomatoes and eggplant. Very lightly salt, if desired, and add fresh ground pepper.

Optional—add a sprinkle of grated Parmesan.

Bake at 175°C/350°F until tomatoes begin to brown/caramelize; approximately 60 to 90 minutes. Raise temperature to 190°C/375°F for 20 minutes. Then lower back to 175°C/350°F. Bake until desired softness of vegetables.

Cut like a pie.

VEGETABLE GRATIN

Start to finish: 2 hours
Serves 6

2 baking potatoes, peeled and sliced
1 yellow squash, sliced
Fresh basil
2 large tomatoes, thinly sliced
1 eggplant, thinly sliced
Sliced onion
Garlic
1 tablespoon lemon juice
Parmesan cheese
Olive oil
Vegetable oil

Fry sliced potatoes and onion in a skillet with 2 tablespoons of vegetable oil, 2 pinches of sea salt, and a generous pinch of fresh ground pepper. Season a 10-inch square baking dish with garlic clove by running a slightly bruised or crushed clove over the bottom and sides of the dish. Leave the crushed garlic in the baking dish.

Lay the fried potato and onion flat in the square baking dish.

Thinly slice the squash. Sauté the squash in the skillet with a bit of olive oil, the lemon juice, and fresh ground pepper for 3 to 5 minutes. Layer squash over potatoes.

Add a bit more vegetable oil to the pan and begin frying eggplant slices. Fry in batches on both sides until brown. Layer over squash. Layer sliced tomatoes over eggplant.

Sprinkle fresh cut basil on top.

Bake for an hour at 175°C/350°F. Remove from the oven and press the vegetables down with a potato masher or large spoon. Sprinkle with 1 cup, or more if desired, of grated Parmesan. Bake for remaining 15 minutes. Turn off oven. Serve warm.

A Summer Place

The Luberon in the Provence region of France has a magnificent beauty, heat, and daytime desolation during the summer months all its own. Marcel Pagnol's description of the mistral and its howling winds that affect the human psyche so profoundly as to not be ignored, come to mind whenever I enter this region. The region's beauty, equally, cannot be ignored.

One summer when my children were small, we rented a house our bastide, in Provence. It captured dreams. Remote, yet not so remote as to deprive visitors of a few essential comforts—a well-stocked local bookstore, good butcher, farmers' market, not-too distant-friends for evening meals, games, dancing, and drinking within a safe drive home. There were no visible neighbors once up the steep, pebbly, tree-lined drive to our favorite house, which ended in the embrace of an enormous willow. The willow's shade was comforting and somehow brushed away the dust and heat after whatever journey brought one to the door.

Days were spent by the pool overlooking the hills that resembled waves of wheat-yellow grass burned by the sun. The courtyard garden of the bastide was an oasis of green thanks to the water source that ran through it. It also kept occupants and the house cool even in the hottest days of summer. Between the willow and the source, we were cocooned and well-protected from the heat.

Throughout our stay, we welcomed visitors, friends, and family from every part of the world passing through the region en route to one festival or another, school, or the coast. A three-day visit always turned into four. The daybed on the courtyard terrace off the sitting room was my favorite resting place after the morning shopping and preparation and enjoyment of the substantial afternoon lunch, the main meal during holidays. I often fell asleep there, lulled by the shade, the trickle of the fountain, and the smells of fresh rosemary, a Provençal staple, along with lavender. My aromatic paradise. Between inhaling and listening to the world around me, I dozed off into a stressless slumber.

STUFFED ZUCCHINI

Reminiscent of summer meals in Provence, the stuffing here can be used as a filling for a variety of summer vegetables—red bell peppers, squash, onions.

Start to finish: 90 minutes
Serves 3 or 6

500g/1lb. extra lean ground beef

½ cup chopped, fresh basil
3 large zucchini
1 medium red onion, finely chopped
2 garlic cloves, crushed
¾ cup curly parsley, finely chopped
1 can chopped tomato
Juice of 1 lemon
Kosher salt

½ teaspoon peppercorns
Herbamare
Balsamic vinegar
¼ cup grated Parmesan cheese
1 slice soft white bread
Cane sugar, a pinch

Olive oil
2 tablespoons whole milk

Sauté the red onion, parsley, and peppercorns in 3 tablespoons of kosher salted olive oil. After 5 minutes, add juice of ½ a lemon. Let simmer for 20 minutes. While this is simmering, prepare the tomato sauce by sautéing chopped garlic, whole basil leaves, and a few peppercorns in olive oil. After 5 minutes, add the tomatoes and a spoonful of lemon juice, a pinch of sugar, and salt to taste. Cover and let simmer.

Once the onion has simmered, let cool. Clean and halve the zucchini lengthwise. Scoop out the white flesh, leaving boat-shaped zucchini. Place the zucchini skin-side up on some aluminum foil. Place the flesh of the vegetable alongside it. Season the vegetables with fresh ground pepper, Herbamare, a light spray of olive oil and juice of half a lemon. Run the vegetable under a broiler to lightly grill the green skin and the flesh. Remove.

Stuffing:
Mash the bread in with the onion. Add about 2 tablespoons of whole milk. Stir in the ground beef and season with salt and pepper. Mix well.

Arrange the zucchini boats flesh-side up in a baking dish. Stuff each boat with about 1 tablespoon of ground meat mixture. Pour the tomato sauce over and top with grated Parmesan cheese. Bake at 200°C/400°F for 30 minutes.

Serve with a green salad topped with a mixture of the grilled zucchini flesh, and any other desired vegetables like string beans and potatoes, tossed with balsamic dressing.

RATATOUILLE
Start to finish: 2 hours
Serves 6–8

4 zucchini, cleaned and cut into 6 pieces
2 medium eggplant, peeled and cut into 8–10 pieces
(*optional*)
2 red bell peppers, deseeded and cut in half
2 yellow or green bell peppers, deseeded and cut in half
(*optional*)
3 garlic cloves, chopped
1 red onion, coarsely chopped
4 plum tomatoes, deseeded and quartered

Nutmeg
Peppercorns

½ cup olive oil, earthy rustic

Set oven to 220°C/425°F before preparing vegetables. I prefer this dish without eggplant and green pepper, but they are traditional ingredients. If using eggplant, once you slice it down, place in a colander and sprinkle on each side with salt. This will remove the bitter juices. Let the eggplant sit in the colander for 20 minutes. After 20 minutes, rinse the eggplant with cold water to remove all of the salt.

Spread all of the vegetables, except the garlic, evenly in a roasting pan. The peppers should be skin-side up. Place about a cup of water in the pan with the vegetables. Roast for approximately 20 minutes. The skin of the tomatoes and peppers should char slightly. When done, remove from the oven. Remove the skin from the peppers. For the tomatoes, you can keep the skin or remove it. Place all of the vegetables in a casserole dish. Add the seasoning (a few peppercorns and grated nutmeg), olive oil, and garlic. Stir and let simmer on the burner for approximately 40 to 60 minutes.

Variations:

RATATOUILLE WITH FETA CHEESE

Add dry feta cubes and chopped chives to leftover ratatouille. If the ratatouille is watery, add some ready-made red pesto to hold it all together.

RATATOUILLE WITH COUSCOUS

Leftover ratatouille mixes nicely with cooked couscous. This can be served with leftover sliced lamb, falafel, or roast chicken, and salad.

When Aren't Eggs Good?

Quiche, like an omelet, is a great way to extend some leftovers into a full meal. If you keep eggs in the fridge, take them out the night before you make the quiche. You want the eggs to be at room temperature when you are ready to make the quiche. The frothier you can make the eggs while whipping, the closer you will get to the custard-like brilliance of French quiches.

QUICHE

The crust is crucial to the satisfaction quotient of any quiche. To make a dough for a 12- to 15-inch pie dish, you need a stick of butter (125g), cold water, 1½ cups of self-rising flour, and a pinch of salt. Take the butter out of the fridge the night before you make the quiche. Mix the flour and butter. Halfway through mixing, add a pinch of salt and 3 tablespoons of cold water. Continue mixing until you have a smooth dough ball. Let chill in the fridge for 10 minutes. Roll out on a flat, floured surface. If calorie conscious, only line the bottom of the quiche dish with the dough. If not, place all of the dough into the quiche dish and roll up the sides and over the edges to form a nice wall of dough around the top of the quiche dish. Pierce the bottom of the quiche dish in a few places with a fork. Bake the dough for about 20 minutes at 170°C/350°F.

Remove from the oven and let cool. If you are buying ready-made dough, I suggest puff pastry rather than short crust. Like homemade dough, you have to roll it out and bake it prior to adding the filling.

In a mixing bowl, crack open 4 room-temperature eggs, add a pinch of salt, and beat until very fluffy. Optionally, you can also take a fifth egg and separate the white that you will beat stiffly to fold into the quiche mix. The fifth yolk can go into the beaten eggs, or not.

Spinach quiche
Add chopped cooked spinach, grated nutmeg, shredded cheese such as Emmental, and fresh ground pepper to the beaten eggs. Fold the ingredients into the egg. If using an extra egg white, now fold that into the well-mixed spinach mixture. Pour into

the quiche crust. Top with a sprinkle of grated cheese. Bake until the top is golden.

Ratatouille quiche
Fold leftover ratatouille into the beaten eggs, along with some grated Parmesan or pecorino cheese. Pour the mixture into the crust. Top with a sprinkle of cheese, followed by thin tomato slices, if desired. Bake for 30 minutes.

Ham, cheese, and onion quiche
Thinly slice one medium yellow onion and sauté in salted butter on medium heat until caramelized. Add 2 cups of diced cooked ham. The ham should not be too lean; ideally, use pieces with a bit of fat that will crisp nicely. Ham, not bacon. Sauté the onions and ham for about 4 or 5 minutes. Let cool. Once cool, mix in with the beaten eggs and add 1 cup of grated Emmental cheese and some fresh ground pepper. A heaping tablespoon of crème fraîche is optional. Mix well and pour into the crust. Bake for 30 minutes or until golden on top.

Serve with a green salad.

SCRAMBLED EGGS
Start to finish: 10 minutes

As simplicity goes, eggs in France were a winner. I especially enjoyed eggs that were scrambled on such a low buttery heat that they resembled a delicate porridge. They nicely topped triangles of toast and were finished with pinches of delicate parsley, chervil, or finely diced chives. Gorgeous comfort food.

2 eggs per person
Salt

Eggs

Heavy cream
Pepper
Butter

Place a nonstick pan over low heat.

Add butter (approximately 4 tablespoons/50g). Lightly salt the pan.

Crack desired amount of fresh eggs into the pan.

Pour cream (whichever type you prefer) over each yolk (about a teaspoon) to coat it.

Season the eggs with salt and pepper as desired.

Begin to slowly whisk the eggs and increase the pan to a medium heat. Some prefer a wooden spoon to a whisk for beating the eggs.

Once the eggs begin to reach desired consistency, reduce the heat to the lowest setting or, better yet, turn off the heat. The pan will still be hot enough to continue cooking the eggs.

For a porridge-type egg, stir vigorously. For a ribbony scramble, continually fold the eggs. Constantly turn the eggs until desired runniness or hardness.

Decidedly, the chicken came first.

Entrées

Thinking back on foods I discovered in France, I realize that so much of the culinary art there is an amalgam. So many of the dishes I enjoyed in France reflect how and why France is the culinary heart of Europe; it has influences from every direction woven into its cuisine. Beef stroganoff, couscous, *macaronade* and *pâtés, baba au rhum, accras de morue, harengs, bavarois, briks, caviar d'aubergines, choucrotte,* taboulé, and coulibiac.

SALMON IN PUFF PASTRY

This recipe is inspired by my love of coulibiac, a Russian dish I first tasted in Paris.

Start to finish: 90 minutes
Serves 8–12

Salmon loin, about a foot long
1 egg

100g/¾ cup of washed and chopped spinach
3 shallots, finely chopped
A bunch of flat parsley or sorrel
The juice of half a lemon

Fresh ground sea salt to taste
Fresh ground pepper to taste
1 chicken bouillon cube

¾ stick of salted butter
Crème fraîche
320g/0.7lbs ready-rolled puff pastry

Boil the egg for three minutes and then cut the heat and leave the egg in the water for 10 minutes. After 10 minutes, remove the egg from the water and set aside.

In a medium skillet, on medium heat, melt the butter and then add the chopped shallots to sauté in the butter; when they start to get caramel brown add the parsley and spinach (to modify, you can also add a few finely diced mushrooms when you add the spinach), season with salt and pepper and continue sautéing on low for about 20 minutes. All of the liquid should evaporate. Add one soft chicken bouillon cube and crush and mix into the mixture while still on the heat.

Slightly increase the temperature and add the lemon juice to the vegetable sauté. The lemon juice will help dissolve the rest of the bouillon cube. Let cook until you are left with a vegetable mixture that is not runny. Remove from the heat and add a heaping tablespoon of crème fraîche (more if you like, and you can use half-fat crème) to the mixture, stirring well.

Peel the boiled egg, crush it with a fork, and add to the vegetable mixture. Let this completely cool down.

Roll out the puff pastry and place the clean, dry salmon loin in the center. Season if you like with a bit of sea salt and pepper. Spread the spinach cream on top of the salmon. Fold one side of the pastry over the salmon and then the other so that the salmon is completely wrapped in the puff pastry. Make some ventilation holes in the pastry with a fork and seal the ends. Decorate with extra dough or brush on egg yolk, as desired. I find that if you use quality all-butter pastry it browns quite nicely. Lastly, short-crust pastry can be used just as well as puff pastry.

Bake according to the pastry instructions, until the pastry is nice and golden, usually 30 to 40 minutes.

France was a portal to many, many happy times along the Mediterranean and Atlantic seaside. The following three mains give a nod to those shores.

SEA BASS IN SALT BRICK

In the South of France, so much pleasure is derived from the presentation of a whole fish baked in a cocoon of sea salt. Sel de Guerande is sea salt that when baked becomes hard, forming a salt shell around the fish and allowing the fish to steam to perfection—meaning the taste of the ocean is sealed in the fish.

Start to finish: 45 to 50 minutes
Serves 4

1 large fresh sea bass or sea bream

Lemons
Fresh herbs

Sea salt for packing, *Sel de Guerande*
Peppercorns

Butter or olive oil

Preheat the oven to 225°C/450°F or its hottest setting, usually around 250°C/475°F.

Clean the fish, which your fishmonger should have already scaled and gutted for you. Remove any trailing scales.

Classic herbs for fish usually involve dill and parsley. You can also try the fine fennel leaves, tarragon, thyme, and chervil, a fine parsley. Because I associate this preparation method with the south of France, I have also used rosemary with my herb mixture. Whichever herbs you choose, roughly chop and mix them with some cracked peppercorns and a pat of butter and then stuff in the cavity of the fish.

Take a baking dish that will comfortably hold the fish. Spread a layer of sea salt on the bottom of the dish. Place the fish on the salt. Thoroughly cover the fish with sea salt. You want to encase the fish in the sea salt. Pat the sides in. The salt should feel tight around the fish. Place in the oven and bake for 30 minutes.

Remove from the oven. The salt will now be hard as a rock. Crack it open and remove the salt. Take a pastry brush to brush the salt off the fish. Peel the skin back to remove the flesh. For show, when you have guests, crack open the salt casing at the dinner table. The fish is wonderful with garlic mashed potatoes and a garnish of olive oil, lemon zest, and chopped parsley. Some lovely green chard leaves provide a perfect side.

BOUILLABAISSE TO FISH SOUP

My first trip to Greece will always be a hallmark in my palate for delicious fisherman's soup. At a dockside cantina one evening, I watched how soup was prepared with the daily catch. There are versions of it throughout the Mediterranean. I think this a soup best tried when you have access to a variety of sustainably-sourced fresh fish. So, it is almost a delicacy. I will never forget the taste. The memory lives on in this little recipe.

Fish—the fresher, the simpler, the better . . .

This list of fish is not exhaustive and excludes shellfish, to which I am allergic. But if you do want to add shellfish, crayfish and/or crabs would be the choice. Choose a minimum of four or five types of seafood to make the soup. Once you have the seafood scaled, gutted, and cleaned, separate it into two plates, one with the firm fish and the other with the delicate fish. Section each fish into three or four pieces. The firm and soft fish will go in the boiling stock in varying stages.

Start to finish: 75–90 minutes
Serves 7–8

Rock fish
Monkfish tail
Snapper
Haddock
John Dory
Red mullet

2 large onions, diced
3–4 garlic cloves
4 tomatoes, deseeded and skinless
1 fennel bulb, trimmed, sliced, coarsely chopped

Flat parsley, about 10 stems
2 potatoes, peeled and sliced 1 inch thick
1 large bay leaf
Pinch or two of lemon zest

Saffron threads
6–8 cups fish stock
Peppercorns
Sea salt

Olive oil

Take a large casserole with a lid; I like Le Creuset, but a good stainless-steel pot is also great. On medium, heat a generous ½ cup of olive oil in the casserole. Add a healthy pinch of salt and then the onions, garlic, tomato, fennel, parsley stems, peppercorns, and bay leaf. Stir well; cover the pot with its lid and let cook for 10 minutes. In a separate saucepan, heat the fish stock that you will use throughout the recipe.

Layer the sliced potatoes on top of the vegetables in the casserole and season with a pinch of salt. Layer the firm fish on top of the potatoes. Add a pinch of salt and lemon zest and a few threads of saffron. Add just enough warm fish stock (or water if you do not have fish stock) to the casserole to cover the fish. Bring this to a boil in a closed casserole. Reduce to medium heat so the stock is still bubbling but you don't risk burning the bottom of the dish.

After 5 minutes, remove the lid and add the tender fish and add more liquid, if necessary, to cover the fish. Replace the lid on the casserole and bring to a low boil again for 5 minutes. Remove the fish from the casserole and arrange it on a serving dish. Keep warm while you finish with the stock.

Let the stock simmer for 5 minutes or more while stirring the ingredients. Remove the bay leaf. Then take a handheld masher and gently crush the vegetables. This will thicken the broth. Let simmer for 20 minutes. To serve, ladle soup into shallow soup bowls and add some of the fish to each bowl or ladle the soup and present the fish on the serving dish. Drizzle the fish with olive oil, and fresh chopped parsley. Of course, serve with a country loaf.

COD IN RED PEPPERS

Biarritz gem.
Start to finish: 1 hour
Serves 4–8

500g/1lb. cod loin

3 garlic cloves
4 potatoes
1 lemon
4 good-size red bell peppers

White pepper
Bouillon cube

Olive oil
Crème fraîche
Parmesan or sheep cheese (*optional*)
Salted butter

Clean, vertically halve, and deseed the red peppers. Place skin-side up on a baking tray. Brush lightly with olive oil and broil until the skin begins to brown. Watch the peppers with a careful eye to avoid burning the skin. Remove from the oven and set aside to cool. Turn them over.

Add 1 bouillon cube to a large saucepan with 1 to 1½ liters of water. Bring to a boil. While this is coming to a boil, peel the skin from the potatoes. Quarter the potatoes and boil with the garlic cloves in the seasoned water until soft. Remove the cooked potatoes and garlic from the water. Place in a bowl. Keep the water in the pan and leave simmering.

Rub a bit of lemon juice over the cod and poach the cod in the potato water. Once cooked through, remove from the water and set aside to cool. Discard the water or freeze it as a fish stock. Return the potatoes and garlic to the pan and place on low heat. Mash the potatoes and garlic. Add the cooked cod and continue mashing until you have a cohesive fish mash. Season with butter, salt, white pepper to taste and stir with a spoon. Remove from the heat. Add a dollop or two of crème fraîche.

Brush the cavities of the red peppers with olive oil and add a pinch of salt. Fill each red pepper with the cod and potato mixture. Form small peaks with the mixture. Then bake to brown the peaks. The tops of the potato can also be topped with a sprinkle of Parmesan or sheep cheese, as desired. I do not add cheese.

VEGETABLE CASSOULET

A French staple from the southwest of the country, cassoulet usually involves duck, pork, and white beans. I make this vegetable cassoulet as a healthier and easier-to-digest version of the traditional stew.

Start to finish: 2 hours 20 minutes
Serves 6
A mixture of vegetables can be used, but a few basics are:

Savoy cabbage or cavalo Nero (black Italian leaf greens)
Baby carrots
Red onion
Spinach
Potatoes
Garlic

Peppercorns
Bay leaf

Duck fat or Olive Oil

Take the raw equivalent of 4 cups of cooked greens. I remove the stems from the greens. Once cleaned, place them in a large stockpot. Turn the heat on to medium. Add about ¼ of a thinly sliced red onion, bay leaf, and 8 to 10 peppercorns. Cook for 20 minutes. Then add 100g/1 cup of chopped spinach leaves, and three carrots cut into fourths. Cover and let simmer for half an hour. Then add the potatoes, halved. Season the potatoes with Herbamare. Let simmer for 30 minutes. In a nonstick skillet, heat 2 to 4 tablespoons of duck fat or olive oil. Remove the potatoes from the casserole. They will be firm, not at all cooked through. Slice each half into about 4 sections. Sauté the potatoes in the duck fat or olive oil on medium heat for 5 minutes—they should be crispy brown on one side. Then season with one crushed garlic clove, a little salt and fresh ground pepper. Stir the garlic and potatoes well. When the garlic hits the duck fat or olive oil you will be in aroma heaven. Enjoy that for a minute, or at least thirty seconds. You don't want the garlic to burn.

Lower the temperature to a low setting and cover. Cook until the potatoes are tender—this takes about 20 minutes.

The greens would have finished cooking down nicely. Serve the potatoes on a plate with the greens.

This goes well with confit duck legs, roast duck, or pork. And crusty French bread.

Variation: Smoked ham hock can be added for a meatier version, and white navy beans for vegans.

SALMON "A L'UNILATERAL" WITH WATERCRESS SAUCE

Start to finish: varies

I love preparing all fish fillets with skin by this method. The one-sided cooking method nicely crisps the skin and leaves very moist flesh. This also works well with sea bass and sea bream fillets.

Salmon side, 600–800g

Olive oil

Make sure all of the scale residue is off the skin by scraping a sharp knife in reverse along the scales. Rinse any stray scales away with cold water. Heat a large skillet on medium. Let it get hot. Lightly brush the pan with a bit of olive oil where the fish will be placed. Place the salmon skin-side down in the skillet. Season the flesh with freshly ground sea salt and pepper if desired. Let cook. Cover the skillet with a lid about halfway through cooking. Check every 5 minutes. The flesh should remain slightly translucent unless, of course, you want it well done. The fish is done when the skin is crispy and easily lifted from the pan. Serve as desired.

NB: Sea bass and sea bream have to cook through—they should not be translucent.

Variation: Sea bass and sea bream work well with light pre-cooking marinades.

Marinades:
• Sumac, lemon juice or lemon zest, and olive oil
• Crushed tomatoes or paste, with Maggi liquid seasoning, and minced green chilis

- Fresh ginger and garlic with chopped cilantro and tamari
- Lemon juice and olive oil with sea salt and pepper
- Tandoori mix powder with strained yogurt

All of these marinades will adhere to the fish and cook well on a grill or under the oven broiler. I often use a *plancha* type cast-iron grill rather than the charcoal fire. If you want the smoky outdoor grill taste you can always add a drop or two of liquid smoke to the marinade. I would use liquid smoke sparingly and highly recommend cooking on the outdoor grill if a wood smoke taste is preferred. If you are using a gas grill you might as well cook on the cast-iron stovetop skillet or *plancha*.

Watercress sauce
Take a handful, 100g or so, of watercress and wilt for 3 minutes in boiling water. Drain, pat dry, and blend with 3 cups of plain yogurt, 2 tablespoons of olive oil, and salt to taste.

MONKFISH IN TOMATO SAUCE

Monkfish, the filet mignon of fish, makes a great dish for special occasions or a treat.

Start to finish: 60 minutes
Serves 4

Monkfish fillet (1½ lbs./700 grams)

1 bunch flat-leaf parsley, finely chopped
I medium size carrot, finely chopped
I small brown onion, finely chopped
1 can chopped tomatoes or 10 fresh, deseeded and diced
Juice of ½ a lemon
Fresh tarragon, julienned to garnish

½ cup cognac
Flour for coating

100g/4 tablespoons of salted butter
3 tablespoons of crème fraîche

Clean the monkfish and remove the tough skin if not already done for you. Slice on the round into 2-inch steaks. Flatten lightly with the back of a spoon. Season one side of each steak with salt and pepper. Then lightly coat each steak in flour. Shake off excess flour and set aside.

Heat the salted butter in a large nonstick skillet over medium-high heat.

Cook the monkfish in the butter for 3 minutes per side. Remove from the butter and set aside in a baking/serving dish. Pour the parsley, carrot, and onion into the same skillet and sauté for 5 minutes. Add any juices that have run off the cooked fish while sitting in the baking dish into the skillet and season with salt and pepper. Raise the heat, stir well, and add the cognac. Stir the vegetables until the cognac evaporates.

Once the liquid has evaporated, stir in the chopped tomatoes. Lower the heat to simmer, cover the pan, and let simmer for 20 minutes.

Stir in the crème fraîche and let simmer for another 20 minutes. Place the monkfish steaks in the sauce side by side, coat with the sauce, and leave to simmer uncovered or partially covered for 20 minutes.

Serve with basmati or Thai jasmine rice and garnish with fresh herbs such as tarragon.

SMOKED SALMON WITH POTATO PANCAKES

A friend and I discussed a cooking show where the host literally opened and plated a pack of smoked salmon, sliced some rustic granary bread, spread it with a lovely butter, and then presented this trio as a dish. My friend asked me how I would serve smoked salmon. Simply is always good, but the question took my thoughts back to my days living in Paris where I came to appreciate smoked salmon, especially a smoked fillet, with potato pancakes during the end-of-year holidays. I offer a version of how to lift smoked salmon when you must.

Start to finish: 30 minutes
Serves 4

Wild smoked salmon

2 large baking potatoes
1 lemon, wedged
Chives, *optional*

Herbamare
Fresh ground pepper
Self-rising flour, *optional*

Sunflower oil
Crème fraîche

Brush, clean, and peel the potatoes. If you do not want to peel the potatoes, place the potatoes in a bowl of hot water and scrub them clean with a brush. Cut out any dark spots. Peeled or not, finely grate the potatoes with a medium-hole cheese grater. If the grate size is too small, the potatoes become sudsy.

Pat the potato shreds dry and season with a very little Herbamare, some fresh ground pepper, and about a tablespoon of minced chives, if using. You do not want to add a lot of Herbamare because the fish is salty and you can actually leave the Herbamare out of the potatoes. Add a tablespoon of flour, if using. Mix well.

Heat about 1 cup of oil in a nonstick skillet. Divide the shredded potatoes into four sections. Take one section of shredded potato in your hand and press it to form a pancake. Do this with each section. Fry each potato cake in the oil until brown on each side. When done, place on a towel to absorb the excess oil.

Serve with smoked salmon and crème fraîche. I spread a bit of crème fraîche on each potato and then layer two pieces of salmon on top. Serve with a lemon wedge.

Variation: Smoked salmon on buckwheat blinis. Replace the potato pancakes with blinis.

Buckwheat blinis:
1 cup buckwheat
½ teaspoon baking soda
1 egg, separated
Pinch of salt
1½ cups oat milk
3 tablespoons/60g of butter

Sift the buckwheat with the baking soda and salt into a bowl.

Place a saucepan on low heat and add the oat milk. Heat for 3 minutes or until it starts to steam. Remove from the heat and beat in the egg yolk. Add the butter as well and stir to melt. Let cool for a few minutes.

Stir the milk from the saucepan into the flour with a spoon. You may need to add ¼ cup more of milk to create a pancake-like batter, with no lumps. Use your judgment with the milk; you may need to drizzle in a bit more. Cover the batter with cling wrap and let sit for 20 minutes. If the batter is stiff, drizzle in a bit more oat milk. In the end you should not require more than 1½ cups of oat milk in total for this recipe.

Beat the egg white until stiff. Fold into the batter when the 20 minutes of sitting time has finished.

Heat a nonstick skillet and add a bit of butter to coat the pan to fry the blinis. Mini-blinis are a level tablespoon of batter per blini. Cook on each side until browned. Cool on a baking rack. The batter should produce over 2 dozen small blinis. Top as desired with salmon. The blinis keep for 2 days in a sealed container in the refrigerator.

FILLETS WITH MUSHROOM RISOTTO

This works nicely with any delicate white fish fillets, such as plaice and sole.

Start to finish: 90 minutes
Serves 4–6

8–12 white fish fillets

Lemons
Chives, chopped
Rosemary, chopped leaves, no stem
12 mushroom caps, finely diced
1 shallot, finely diced
1 garlic clove, finely diced
1 cup chopped parsley
Crème fraîche

White wine
Apple cider vinegar
2 cups of uncooked risotto rice
2 chicken bouillon cubes

Salted butter

This dish requires a large soufflé dish. Preheat the oven to 190°C/375°F.

For the mushroom arborio, sauté the mushrooms, shallot, garlic, and chopped parsley on medium-high in 3 table-spoons of salted butter in a deep saucepan with a lid. Heat and melt the butter before adding those vegetables and herbs.

After 15 minutes, once the water from the mushrooms has started to evaporate, splash with ½ cup of white wine. Stir and continue cooking for a few minutes. Add bouillon cubes; stir well, then add the boiling water. Mix well so that the bouillon melts. Add the arborio rice. Stir well so that the rice is evenly covered with liquid. Bring to a quick boil, cover, and reduce to a very low heat. Leave to cook for 20 minutes. Ideally, cook the fish while the rice is cooking.

Clean the fish, pat dry, and roll each fillet into a pinwheel and place around the rim of the soufflé dish. The pinwheels should have a nice round opening because you will fill each with rice pilaf. Season with salt and pepper or Herbamare and pour about 1 cup of white wine over the fillets. Bake in the preheated oven for 20 minutes, close to the time you want to serve. You can arrange the fish in the dish ahead of time and chill until ready to cook.

For the sauce, chop ¼ cup of chives and the same of rosemary. Sauté in 100g of salted butter for 10 minutes. Season to taste with salt, pepper, and the juice of one lemon. Whisk in a tablespoon of apple cider vinegar. When the fish is done cooking, pour the juice from the soufflé dish into this herb sauce and whisk. Increase temperature to a boil and whisk until water has evaporated and you are left with a reduction. Add 1 tablespoon of crème fraîche.

Arrange the fish wheels on a plate, stuff them with the rice, and coat them with the herb sauce.

SALMON AND TAGLIATELLE

My eldest son loved this staple on Parisian café menus, which resulted in the recipe below.

Start to finish: an hour or less
Serves 4

    Organic wild salmon fillets with skin (1–1½ pounds)
Juice of one lemon
1 large, long, finely chopped shallot
1 cup chopped flat-leaf parsley

                                           Fresh pasta

Butter
Olive oil
1 cup crème fraîche
2 cups of single cream

Place clean salmon in a glass baking dish. Pour lemon juice over the salmon. Season with sea salt and fresh ground pepper. Set aside.

In a large skillet, sauté the shallot and parsley in 6 tablespoons of butter for about 10 minutes. Spoon up some of the lemon juice from the salmon dish and add to shallots. Let cook for 2 more minutes.

Place salmon fillets skin-side down in the pan with the shallots, pushing them aside to make room for the salmon. Cover the skillet; reduce the heat and leave to cook for 15 minutes. Carefully remove the salmon from the pan and set it aside; discard the skin.

Pour the creams into the skillet, mix well with the shallots, and season with salt and pepper. Cook for 5 minutes. Cook fresh tagliatelle or fettuccine for four in water seasoned with salt and olive oil. Remove the skillet from the heat and add the salmon to the cream sauce. Stir to break up the fish in the sauce.

Serve over the pasta.

ROAST CHICKEN
Start to finish: 2 hours

One of the best things about any town or city in France is the readily available rotisserie chicken, *poulet roti*. The all-glass and steel frame rotisseries are placed at the storefront, usually on the sidewalk, a couple of hours before noon. The aromas, dripping golden brown juices, and carousel feel of the spits turning and churning are a call to forks, knives, and bellies. Granted, some are tastier than others, but what makes them all so special is their tenderness and locked-in juiciness. The meat comes off the bone with the pull of a fork. The knife is just there by force of habit; it is not really needed to dig into the bird. Nice memories.

In a bowl, add and mix together 1 tablespoon/equal amounts of rosemary, salt, pepper, thyme, Ma Bell's poultry seasoning, and garlic powder.

Clean 1 bird and remove any stray pinfeathers. Dry off and place in a baking dish. Rub the chicken all over the skin with the herb mixture. Slice down the butter and place as much as possible between the skin and flesh; about ½ a stick of butter (56.5g). Turn the bird so that it is in the roasting pan breast-side down. Add 2 cups of water to the pan. Place in a hot oven (220°C/425°F) for 20 minutes. After 20 minutes turn the bird over breast-side up and roast at 175°C/350°F for 1 hour. Baste the chicken and turn the oven off.

Leave the chicken in the oven for another 20 to 30 minutes. Serve with French fries, a green salad, and a quality Dijon mustard.

Tip: Use any leftover chicken to make tetrazzini. Stew the carcass in ½ liter of water to get a broth and remove all the meat. Chop a carrot, celery stalk, some parsley, sage leaves, a bay leaf, and a few peppercorns and sauté in a large skillet in 1 tablespoon of salted butter. Once the onions start to brown, add 1 cup of dry white wine. Let that reduce and add the chicken. Whisk a cup of the broth into 1 level tablespoon of flour in a small bowl. Completely dissolve the flour. Pour over the chicken and vegetables, and stir well. Add a cup of light cream. Reduce the heat to simmer.

Bring the remaining broth and a liter of water to a boil. Add a bit of olive oil. Use to cook the spaghetti (or whichever pasta you prefer). When done, drain and add to the chicken skillet.

The spaghetti quantity should not overwhelm the chicken or sauce. The balance between the spaghetti and the chicken will depend on how much leftover chicken was on hand. Pour into a baking dish and top with an equal mixture of breadcrumbs and Parmesan cheese. Bake at 170°C/350°F for 20 to 30 minutes. Serve with a green salad.

CHICKEN IN BÉCHAMEL SAUCE
(French smothered chicken)
Stewed chicken pieces harken back to my grandmothers' dining tables. Combining the comfort of stew gravy with French béchamel came naturally and found its way into this recipe.

Start to finish: 100 minutes
Serves 6

Whole chicken

Mushrooms
Leek
Flat parsley

Dry white wine (worthy of the table—
I like a dry white Vouvray)
Ma Bell's poultry seasoning
2 juniper berries
1 bay leaf
Flour
Colman's mustard powder
Celery salt

Heavy cream
Butter
Grated Gruyère/Swiss cheese *(optional)*

Clean and cut chicken into eight pieces. Place in a bowl that you can later cover or in Tupperware.

Place a deep skillet on low to medium heat and add ½ stick salted butter and the juniper berries. Let the butter melt.

While the butter is melting, take a large bowl where you will put the bird. Season the chicken pieces with celery salt, pepper, poultry season-all (I like Ma Bell's), 1 teaspoon of mustard powder, and 2 tablespoons of flour. Cover and shake so that the chicken pieces are coated.

By now the butter should be hot. Remove the juniper berries and set aside for later.

Brown the chicken in the butter on each side. You may have to do this in batches.

The container that held the chicken should have coating left in it. Add the water to the container to whisk up all of the flour coating left. This will give a nice thickening sauce to be used later.

While the chicken is browning, chop/dice, not slice, the 12 mushrooms, 1 leek, and a small bunch of parsley. When the chicken is browned, remove from the pan and place in a deep baking dish.

Sauté the mushrooms for 10 minutes in same pan. This should remove the water from the mushrooms by evaporation. Add the leek, parsley, juniper berries, and bay leaf to the mushrooms and sauté until the total starts to become tender (about 7 minutes). Once sautéed, raise the temperature to high and add 1 cup of dry white wine. Let the liquid bubble up and then reduce the temperature. While that is bubbling, pour ⅓ cup of the white wine into a glass and drink it (if you like).

Add the flour mixture to the pan and cook for 5 minutes. Add the cream (1 to 1½ cups), stir, and place the chicken pieces back in the cream sauce. Let simmer on low for 20 minutes.

Place the chicken pieces back in the table-ready ovenware baking dish. Add 1 tablespoon of grated cheese to the sauce and whisk it into the sauce. Pour the sauce over the chicken in the baking dish. Garnish with a bit of grated cheese if desired and bake for a further 20 minutes.

Serve with steamed rice or mashed potatoes and the dry white wine, of course.

SPANISH TWIST ON ROAST CHICKEN

From Valencia, to Jávea, to Malaga, this coastal Spanish stretch holds more than tapas and paella.

Start to finish: 1 hour 40 minutes
Serves 4–6

1 chicken

Salt
Black pepper
Paprika
Cumin
Garlic powder
Thyme
1 yellow onion, finely sliced
1 red pepper, sliced
1 green or orange pepper, sliced
4 baking potatoes, peeled and sliced or quartered
3 garlic cloves

Saffron threads
1 cup chicken bouillon *(optional)*

Olive oil

Butterfly or cut a roaster into eight pieces. With the tip of a sharp knife, pierce the flesh all over. In a small bowl, combine salt and black pepper to taste, ¾ teaspoon each of paprika, cumin, garlic powder, and 1½ to 2 teaspoons of thyme. Rub the seasoning into the skin of the chicken. In a baking dish, arrange fine slices of green pepper, onion, red pepper, and ½- to 1-inch slices of baking potatoes. Season with 3 diced garlic cloves, salt, and pepper to taste, ⅓ cup of olive oil, and saffron threads. Saffron is precious, but I use a good liberal pinch. Toss to mix the flavors. Arrange the chicken pieces on top of the potato and pepper mix. Bake in the oven at 220°C/425°F for 20 minutes and then 170°C/350°F for 1 hour. Baste during cooking, if you like, with 1 cup of chicken bouillon. I highly recommend the basting.

Turn the oven off. Remove the dish from the oven. Place the chicken on a plate, cover with foil, and let sit for 10 minutes or so. During this time, return the roasting pan with the vegetables to the oven to keep warm. Serve with crusty rustic bread.

CHICKEN BREAST FILLETS IN MUSTARD CREAM SAUCE

Start to finish: 45–60 minutes
Serves 8

8 chicken breasts
Dry white wine
1 generous tablespoon Dijon mustard
1 teaspoon garlic powder
2 teaspoons Ma Bell's poultry seasoning
½ cup flour
White pepper

Duck fat (*optional*)
Olive oil
Peanut oil
2 generous tablespoons crème fraîche
½ cup single cream

Butterfly and flatten the breasts with a mallet. In a small bowl, mix the garlic powder, salt, fresh ground pepper, Ma Bell's, and flour. Lightly flour the chicken pieces with this seasoned flour.

I like to pan-fry the fillets in a shallow coating of duck fat. Alternatively, use an oil combination of ¼ cup olive oil and ⅛ cup peanut oil. Season the oil with a few pinches of salt. Brown the breasts on each side and set aside in a baking dish. Place in a warm oven while you prepare the sauce.

There should be a crispy, floury residue left in the skillet where you browned the chicken. Increase to medium heat and whisk in a heaping tablespoon of Dijon mustard. Continue whisking and add a cup of dry white wine, like Vouvray. Heat to a bubbly reduction, and then add 2 heaping tablespoons of crème fraîche and ½ cup of heavy cream. Season to taste with salt and white pepper. Reduce the heat to low. Stirring, let bubble and reduce a bit.

Add the juice from the chicken and the chicken breasts to the sauce. Let simmer for a few minutes.

Serve with garlic mashed potatoes and mixed vegetables.

STUFFED LAMB SHOULDER

For a special Sunday roast lunch, this lamb dish is a standout.

Start to finish: up to 2 hours
Serves 6–8

1 boneless lamb shoulder

1 medium eggplant
1 cup chopped parsley
2 garlic cloves, chopped
1 long shallot, chopped
Fresh rosemary
Lemon zest

1 cup fresh breadcrumbs
1 tablespoon ground cumin

Olive oil

Unroll and clean the shoulder. Place on a work surface. Pierce the interior flesh in several places with a sharp knife. Do the same on the skin side. Bruise some rosemary sprigs by rubbing between your palms, then rub into the flesh and skin. Season both sides with salt and fresh ground pepper. Place the bruised sprigs on the flesh, roll up the lamb shoulder, place in a baking dish, cover, and let sit in the fridge.

Stuffing
Remove the ends of the eggplant. Dice the eggplant, place in a sieve and season with salt. Let that sit for 20 minutes. The bitter juices will run out.

Take a medium-size saucepan that will hold all of the eggplant and place on medium heat. Add a couple of tablespoons of olive oil, a pinch of salt, the shallot, garlic, and parsley. Stir and cook on a low heat while the eggplant is in the sieve. After 20 minutes, rinse all of the salt off the eggplant. Pat dry and add to the saucepan. Increase the heat to a frying temperature; add a bit more olive oil if needed so that the eggplant can fry for up to 5 minutes. Reduce the heat to low, cover the saucepan, and let the eggplant mixture cook for 20 minutes or so. The eggplant should be soft, almost disintegrating. Once done, remove from the heat and let cool. Mix the breadcrumbs with the eggplant mixture. Season to taste with salt and fresh ground pepper.

Remove the lamb from the fridge 1 hour before you are ready to roast it. Preheat the oven to 210°C/400°F. Unroll the lamb and remove the rosemary sprigs. Leave on the side.

Spread the eggplant stuffing inside the lamb. Roll the lamb closed. You may need string to tie the lamb so that it remains closed during roasting. Once back in the baking dish, or if still there, rub the cumin all over the lamb skin. If desired, place tomatoes around the lamb and scatter the rosemary around the pan too. Lightly salt and pepper, drizzle with olive oil. Add the water to the pan.

Place the baking dish with the lamb in the oven. Bake 20 minutes then reduce the oven temperature to 160°C/325°F. Slow roast for 40 minutes to an hour, depending on how well done you want the meat. When done, garnish with tomatoes and pinches of lemon zest.

COUSCOUS STUFFED CHICKEN

Another nod to the crossroads of France, this recipe has a zesty infusion of North African influences.

Start to finish: 3 hours, 2½ hours cooking time
Serves 4–6

1 chicken

2 small onions
6 preserved (*confit*) lemons
½ cup of fresh chopped parsley (*optional*)

3 cups cooked medium-grain couscous or
4 cups fine grain couscous
2 tablespoons leftover onion raisin relish
4 cups hot water
1 chicken bouillon cube
Ma Bell's poultry seasoning

½ stick/56.5g salted butter

Preheat oven to 220°C/425°F.

Heat 1 cup of the water and pour it onto the relish.

Clean the bird, pat dry, and season the cavity with salt and pepper.

In a large bowl mix the moist relish with the cooked couscous and set aside.

Cut the onions in half and then thinly slice each half into crescent-shaped slices.

Stuff the bird with the couscous mixture.

Season the skin of the stuffed bird to taste with salt, pepper, and Ma Bell's. Close the cavity of the bird with a string to prevent the couscous from escaping from the cavity during cooking. Layer the bottom of a large baking dish with the sliced onions. Place the chicken on top. Pat the skin with butter. Bake breast-side down for 20 minutes. Reduce the oven temperature to 170°C/350°F, then remove the chicken from the oven and turn so that it is breast-side up. Add 2 cups water and the 6 confit lemons to the pan. Return to the oven and continue baking for 1 hour, 10 minutes. Toward the end of the chicken cooking time, take a small saucepan and bring the remaining cup of water to a boil and stir in the bouillon cube. Remove from the heat.

Remove the chicken from the oven. Take the lemon, the onion, and all juices and scrapings from the baking dish and add to the bouillon saucepan. Bring the bouillon to a quick boil and then down to a low heat to simmer for 20 minutes. You can cut the confit lemons in half. When done, place 2 lemons in a shallow bowl. Crush the lemons and then rub them over the cooked chicken.

Serve the stuffed chicken with a vibrant green salad. The bouillon, onion, and lemon sauce can be served alongside to moisten the couscous.

Desserts

*One Sunday lunchtime, husband goes into a Chinese restaurant
to collect his family's umpteenth takeout order. The restaurant
owner, upon greeting the husband again, wryly says,*
"Oh, doesn't your wife cook?"
Husband replies,
"Of course she cooks; she just doesn't cook Chinese food."

Things you don't know how to do or make, leave for those
who do. Living in France, I did not need to address my pastry
baking skills. While the French are known for their baguette
and exceptional breads, I fell for the desserts and have sweet
memories, particularly of the French pastry shops. I do not
enjoy making desserts but improvise as needed and otherwise
buy. This selection is for the non-bakers.

FOUR-FOURTHS
(or, The Only Cake I Can Make)
Prep time: 20 minutes

I consider this staple cake recipe I learned in France to be the
equivalent of the American pound cake. This recipe is incred-
ibly simple and so versatile. It consists of four ingredients in
equal measure and is foul (not fool) proof: eggs, flour, sugar,
and butter. It is a confidence builder and can be expanded on
with other ingredients.

3 medium eggs, at room temperature

1 lemon, for the zest

White sugar
Self-rising flour

Vanilla extract
Salt

Soft butter

Preheat the oven to 180°C/350°F. Take a food-weight measuring scale and weigh 3 medium eggs. Whatever their weight, measure out the same weight of butter, sugar, and flour each.

Mix the soft butter and sugar in a large mixing bowl. Add a teaspoon of vanilla extract and a quick grate of lemon zest. Vanilla bean pods can be used in place of extract.

Separate the egg whites from their yolks. Mix the yolks into the sugar-butter mixture and keep the whites in a deep bowl for beating. Always wash your hands with soap and hot water after handling eggs.

Slowly add the flour to the butter, sugar, and yolk mixture. Mix well. Add a pinch of salt to the egg whites and beat until stiff.

Fold the whites into the batter with a plastic spatula or wooden spoon, ⅓ of the batter at a time. This will leave you with a basic cake batter. Pour into a loaf pan and bake for 40 minutes.

MARBLE CAKE

If you can recall the best chocolate ice cream you have ever had, that is what the chocolate mixture for this marble cake should smell like. It should take you back to the moment in your childhood (or adulthood) when your tongue is out, poised to lick, with the tip of your nose a hair's width away from the ice cream, and that aroma memory comes back to you. So, use really good chocolate for the marble mix. I like an organic powdered chocolate.

Prep time: 1 hour 15 minutes or so
Serves 6

2 tablespoons plain yogurt
2 teaspoons powdered chocolate
Batter for the Four-Fourths cake

For the marbling mixture, mix the runny plain yogurt, chocolate powder, and 2 or 3 teaspoons of batter in a bowl. Set aside.

Pour the cake batter into a nonstick small loaf pan. Now drizzle the marble mixture on top of the batter and down the center.

Take a flat spatula and cut the chocolate mix into the batter; have another spatula at hand to get the excess chocolate off the cutting spatula. So, you will push the chocolate mixture down into the batter with the spatula. This gesture of cutting is quite personal. I cut the spatula in at one spot and then twirl the spatula to mix the chocolate batter with the vanilla batter.

When finished marbling the batter, put the pan in the oven. Bake for 40 minutes. The last few minutes you must watch the batter to monitor the absorption of moisture and ensure the cake does not overcook.

APPLE CAKE

An excellent use for those unused apples.

Prep time: 40 minutes
Serves 6–8

Peel and dice 4 apples. Sauté in butter, a pinch of salt, and seasonings if desired. Seasoning could be 1 tablespoon of brown sugar, a teaspoon of vanilla extract, lemon zest, cloves, and cinnamon. I prefer my apples plain and simple. Preheat oven to 180°C/350°F.

Once soft, pour into the bottom of the cake pan. Remove cloves if they were used. Pour the batter for the Four-Fourths cake over the fruit and bake for 40 minutes.

Variations: The batter can also be mixed with pistachio and zucchini. Crush ¼ cup of nuts and mix with ¼ cup of finely grated zucchini. Mix with the batter and bake.

Or, sauté 2 cups of crushed pineapple in 1 tablespoon of butter and brown sugar until the water evaporates. Spread on the bottom of a loaf or round cake pan. Pour the batter over and bake for 40 minutes.

BAKED PEARS

If a cake is simply too challenging under all circumstances, baked fruit almost feels like baking a dessert.

Start to Finish: 90 minutes
1 pear per person

Golden raisins, diced, 1 teaspoon per pear
Lemon juice

Ginger bread
Brown sugar, 1 teaspoon per pear
Vanilla extract

Vanilla ice cream
Salted butter

Preheat the oven to 200°C/400°F.

Peel the pears, taking care to leave the stem intact, and core. Scoop a bit more than the core out of the pear. Slice the bottom of the pear to create a flat bottom so that it will stand up in the baking dish.

Mix the raisins with softened butter. Take approximately 1 teaspoon of raisin and butter each per pear.

Stuff the hollowed-out pear with the raisins.

Arrange in a glass baking dish and drizzle lemon juice over the fruit.

Mix 1 cup of hot water with 1 tablespoon of brown sugar and 1 teaspoon of vanilla extract and pour it in the dish with the fruit.

Bake in the preheated oven for 1 hour. The fruit will render quite a bit of juice and requires basting during the process. You can bake longer at a lower temperature.

Serve with a scoop of vanilla ice cream and a slice of ginger-bread or candied ginger.

Part 3

AFRICA

REVERSE PASSAGES

R oughly three years into life in France, my newlywed
period was abruptly interrupted by a call from Africa
that would add another layer to my food journey. One evening, cozily cocooned at a table in a Paris restaurant with
low lights and velvet trimmings, discussing our day, where
we belong in the world, and our future, my then-husband's
phone rang. Intriguingly, it was a call from a number in Côte
d'Ivoire, his country of birth. Answering with respectful curi-
osity, he received news that would change our trajectory. The
call finished. There was a pregnant pause and I was eager for
a debrief of the call. He was offered a career opportunity in
Africa, long the source of our dreams. The feeling in the air
was as if our conversations and dreams had been overheard
and listened to. The call seemed more than a coincidence. The
opportunity to move there, to return, seemed a quickening.
Damned be the naysayers. We went, giving up the safety of
rewarding careers commensurate with our educational attain-
ments and what was expected. Over the next six years, I would
call Côte d'Ivoire home, give birth to my children there, and
experience many journeys between West and North Africa,
Europe, and North America.

Saharan Beyond

Outside my plane window, the skies were peppered with white and gray clouds that slowly began to change hue. Gray overcame white, and then, within a minute, yellowy brown clouds appeared, while those beyond and ahead were a dirty red. Auburn skies with the light blue canopy told me I was almost home.

Flying over the Sahara felt like crossing an inner threshold, from North to South, from the known to the unknown, from safety to adventure; each crossing would shake me deeply. Elated, I turned my head away from the window to smile at the passenger seated beside me, who, too, had been looking outward, watching the telltale change in the skies.

"We are in Africa now," he said with a forced smile.

I noticed the skin between his heavy brows pinching into a worried frown that made me wonder what awaited him on landing. Arriving during the harmattan season, when the Sahara unrelentingly blows its choking sands everywhere for months on end, I had to ask the same of myself.

Exiting the plane, hazy sunshine and a wall of humidity greeted me with a jolt as soon as I reached the threshold of the plane door. As I walked down the stairs to the tarmac, the intense humidity softening the fabric of my clothes felt like a moist handkerchief dabbing at my face. My hair reacted at the roots, slowly curling up close to my scalp. During the short walk to the terminal building, the sticky air was full of the smell of water-starved, rotting mangroves, belying efforts to classify the giant swamp as a lagoon.

I was home.

Moving to West Africa and a harsh coastal climate, I did not imagine that I was embarking on a food adventure or that just as the markets and pastry shops in Paris lured me in, so too would the culinary delights of my new home during my six years living there. Equally, it was often assumed that I was a native-born sub-Saharan African. While I may have looked African to some, and certainly wanted to live the same, I asked myself whether I could become so. I came to the realization that cooking was one of my ways of becoming a part of the new cultures I found myself in by marriage and forging my identity therein.

Having a home where people ate well was as golden as giving birth to sons.

Just as in Paris, the markets were a part of the food seduction. We lived in Abidjan, a vibrant expanse of city around a lagoon. I loved my local market (*marché*), the colorful fabrics and woven baskets, the well-worn floor, the cloud of tiny dust particles surrounding the perimeters, kicked up by the constant comings and goings of trucks, children, wives, drivers, house girls, the mingling of putrid, sweet, and bloody smells alongside the calm of the vendors, the cool interior. This was the *marché de Cocody*. On the other side of the lagoon was the *marché de Treichville*, hot inside and out, pulsating with movement and music, smells; it was a vaster maze offering up a greater variety of foods and excitement.

On one of my earliest drives out to the Treichville market, I noticed men along the roadside fanning smoke billowing up from mounds of earth. I learned that these mounds were earth pits—ovens—slowly tenderizing lamb, seasoned with spices that I imagined had, throughout time, come in with caravans of traders from the north.

Once at the market, I was greeted by the stall vendors as "auntie" or "maman" as I stopped to fill my food list. Smell is my strongest sensory perception so the aromas also served as a guide. Piles of root vegetables and tubers, with their earthy musk, captured my attention, as did aromatic tomatoes, so sweet and tasty, a reminder they are a fruit, pyramids of fragrant mango, papaya, and the elongated sweet pineapples from the interior of the country. There was an array of dried sea foods, and ocean fish fresh and grilled within hours if not minutes of its catch, succulent and always perfectly sea-salty. This was the norm. I saw the breadth of lived experiences at the market as well.

On one occasion, making my way back to my car through fellow shoppers near the car park, hands full with my daily shop, I heard a woman cry out, "*Hey, voiture là est* sorcière!" "Hey, that car, there is a witch!"

Wearing a cotton *pagne* wrapped around and fixed at her waist with a horizontally striped short-sleeved T-shirt tucked neatly in its folds, the woman was pointing her finger at my car parked on the edge of the market. I had nonchalantly started the motor remotely as I approached it from behind her. Seeing the vehicle light up without human intervention elicited the woman's response that the car was a witch. When I passed in front of her she saw me with the car key, the reassuring smiles of the market bystanders, and waved me on, knowing nothing was amiss. Parallel worlds and realities converged at the market. My market outings were one way that kept me in touch with the pulse of the communities.

One evening, a good family friend stopped by our home around dinnertime. Naturally, he was invited to stay for the meal. I immediately excused myself to escape to the kitchen to make sure I had "enough" food, as I usually only cooked for the number anticipated. He smiled and stopped me from leaving the conversation.

"In Africa, we share whatever is at the table. If there are few, we will eat too much, and if there are many, we will have smaller portions."

There is always enough. This reminded me of my grandparents' table on the other side of the Atlantic decades before. Although worlds apart, just as it was then, the bounty is in the gathering. I have found this to be true as far as I have traveled in each direction on this planet. And how nice that as much as things were new to me, many aspects of life were familiar. While loving the discovery of the new, I always look for the touchstone of what is familiar.

My West African–inspired main-dish recipes are versions that can be prepared and enjoyed just about anywhere. In the spirit of "making do," my recipes use substitutes for the distinct flavors—such as wood charcoal, intense green leaves, dried shrimp, or slice of a giant snail—reminiscent of so many wonderful dishes I sampled throughout living in and traveling this magnificent continent. Luckily, condiments such as Maggi Seasoning Liquid or *Maggi Arome* are now widely available. While I only use it in cooking, I have known those who carry their own supply of Maggi to "lift" a dish; similar to many a handbag's traveling Tabasco stash.

Salads—Starters—Soups

BLACK-EYED PEA FRITTERS

Delicious as an afternoon snack, like *aloco* (fried plaintain), I enjoyed these fritters then and sometimes for breakfast.

Start to finish: 30 minutes
Serves 4

1½ cups dried black-eyed peas
¼ large white onion, chopped
1 tablespoon grated fresh ginger
Salt
⅛ teaspoon cayenne pepper

½ to ¾ cup water

Vegetable oil for frying

Place peas in a bowl, cover with boiling water by at least 2 inches, cover, and soak overnight. Twenty-four hours of soaking is even better. After soaking, drain the liquid and rub peas between hands to remove the skin. This is the most time-consuming part of the recipe. Rinse and strain the peas.

In a food processor, blend the peas with the onion, ginger, salt, cayenne, and ½ cup of water. Process to a smooth paste, adding drips of water as needed but do not exceed ¾ cup of water in total.

Heat the oil, and season it with a bit of salt. Drop the pea batter by teaspoonful into the hot oil. It will take about 5 minutes to fry, 2 or more minutes or so per side. The peas should fry until golden brown. Remove from the oil and place on paper towels to soak up excess oil.

These can be eaten with a simple cooked tomato sauce or on their own.

Variation: Blend the peas with some chopped scallions or jalapeño, salt, and pepper.

HARIRA

Harira, which I first tasted in Morocco, is a soup for the gods. The hefty rich lamb stock and onions, and black pepper heat, is satisfyingly chased by tart lemon juice.

Start to finish: 2½ hours
Serves 4–6

Leftover lamb leg and its gravy

4 cups chopped coriander/cilantro
3 small brown onions, one diced, 2 whole
1 bunch of curly parsley, chopped
Lentils
Chickpeas
3 lemons
1 kilogram deseeded, chopped tomatoes

Saffron
12 Peppercorns

Olive oil

Take a large soup casserole and heat the olive oil on medium heat. Lightly salt and brown the onions. Then add the bone with marrow from the lamb leg if available. Add the chopped tomatoes, saffron, peppercorns, parsley, chickpeas, and juice of 1 lemon, salt, and 2 cups of chopped cilantro. Cover the casserole with a tight lid and let simmer for an hour. After an hour, the marrow should slide out of the bone. Leave the marrow in the sauce, and remove any bits you can. Set the bone aside.

Chop up the lamb leg into bite-size pieces. Add the lamb and its gravy to the casserole, along with the lentils. Salt to taste. Let simmer, uncovered, for another hour.

Add the rest of the lemon juice and cilantro. The whole onions should have almost disintegrated. Where you have whole onion, take a potato masher and gently mash the whole onion in the soup. This will help to thicken the broth. Harira is a hearty soup, so should not be too liquid. Serve as a main.

PEPPER SALAD

This salad is reminiscent of bell pepper spreads and garnishes found in Morocco as starters before a main. Perfect on pitas and sourdoughs.

Start to finish: 30 minutes
Serves 4

Chopped parsley
Pulp of 1 preserved lemon (*confit*), no skin
1 crushed garlic clove
4–6 bell peppers

1 small spoonful chili powder

1 tablespoon groundnut oil

Cut the peppers in half and remove the seeds and white flesh. Grill the peppers under a broiler, remove the skin, which can be discarded, then chop the flesh.

Place in a large saucepan. Add the other ingredients. Let all the ingredients stew on a low heat for 15 minutes, then chill.

Serve with sesame-crusted bread.

MOROCCAN CARROT AND OLIVE SALAD

This salad is a partner to the pepper salad. It whets the palate, not too heavily, before the main dish.

Start to finish: 45 minutes
Serves 4

2 cups carrots, sliced into ½ inch discs
4 small peeled garlic cloves
2 cups potatoes, cut into cubes up to ¾ inches
1 cup chopped fresh coriander/cilantro
¼ cup chopped fresh parsley
1 cup of coriander/cilantro-spiced green, pitted olives
½ cup dried black olives *(optional)*
Juice of ½ lemon

2 teaspoons cumin powder
1 teaspoon chili powder

1 cup olive oil

Bring 1 liter/4 cups of water to a boil, then add the potatoes and garlic cloves. When the potatoes are soft, remove them from the water with a sieve spoon, and set them aside in a bowl to cool. The garlic remains in the water. Boil the carrots in the same water. You may need to top up with a cup of boiling water. Strain the carrots and garlic when done, and let cool.

Once the vegetables and garlic have cooled down a bit, mix all of the ingredients together in a glass bowl. Salt to taste, adding a bit of fresh ground pepper. You may want to mash the soft garlic so that it thoroughly mixes in with the ingredients. The olive quantity can be more or less a cup. If using both black and green olives, take ½ cup of each. Let marinate for at least a few hours. The longer the marinating time, the better the flavors. Serve at room temperature.

BEEF SALAD
Start to finish: 20 minutes
Serves 4

400g/3 cups of leftover cooked beef steak, diced

½ cup chopped flat-leaf parsley
2 cups cooked corn kernels
½ cup diced shallots
Bibb, or similar, lettuce, whole leaves
1 large garlic clove, crushed

Dijon mustard
Fresh ground pepper

Salted butter
1 cup diced Emmental cheese
Olive oil

Heat a medium skillet and add 25g/1 tablespoon of salted butter to sauté 1 can of corn or 2 cups of fresh corn kernels, with 1 chopped garlic clove, shallots, and flat parsley. Season to taste with fresh ground pepper. Cook until the corn is tender and the shallots translucent. Set aside and let cool.

After cooling, mix the corn, beef, and cheese. Serve with mustard and olive oil vinaigrette.

For homemade vinaigrette, whisk a teaspoon of Dijon mustard with ¼ cup of olive oil. Toss with beef, cheese, and corn.

Prepare a dish with lettuce and arrange the beef composition in the center of each leaf.

This beef salad reminds me of my aunt's story of her uncles coming to her home in the 1950s near the end of dinner one day, when she was a newlywed, to find her poised to scrape the gravy from the meat frying pan into the waste bin. They startled her with the cry, "Don't throw away that gravy."

She stopped, and they handily finished the gravy off with some bread. From whence meals come; we always have enough.

Leftovers, or not

What remains today
Should never be thrown away
Serve it well again

Remember, don't throw away the gravy.

LENTIL SALAD
Start to finish: 30 minutes or less
Serves 4–6

Diced ham or garlic sausage
4 cups cooked lentils

½ cup finely diced shallots
½ cup chopped parsley
½ cup deseeded and chopped tomatoes
Garlic clove, grated *(optional)*
½ cup finely chopped celery

1 level tablespoon Dijon mustard

Olive oil
Greek yogurt or mayonnaise (as desired)

Decision to make: if using meat, halve the amount of lentils. So, for 1 cup of lentils, have ½ cup of meat. If using garlic sausage, do not add grated garlic.

Mix all of the ingredients up to mustard in a bowl and sparsely drizzle with olive oil. Bind with Greek yogurt or mayonnaise as desired. It is always nice to let the flavors mingle for a few hours before serving if possible.

Serve on lettuce or sliced tomatoes with crusty rustic bread.

RAW TOMATO AND FRESH THYME "PIZZA"

Thinly slice ripened tomatoes of choice. Spread in a pizza size layer, sprinkle with fresh thyme leaves, paper-thin sliced shallots *(optional)*, drizzle with lemon juice and olive oil, then lightly salt and pepper. Let marinate.

CARROT SALAD

Fresh organic carrots, say 8, scrubbed clean and grated. Grating sizes vary, so choose the texture you like. Add ¼ cup lemon juice. Clean and finely chop one scallion. Sauté the scallion for about 5 minutes in a bit of olive oil. Lightly salt during the cooking. Let cool. Mix the scallion with the carrots. You can add some of the carrots to the pan you cooked the scallion in to pick up the flavor left in the pan. When ready to serve, sparingly add your dressing of choice.

Entrées

The Atlantic Ocean is cold and dark, full of turbulence. For some, it is darkened by a history evidenced by its bone-paved seabed. I thought—I believed—going to Africa was my way of reversing the legacy of the forced passage of some ancestors west, to the Americas, hundreds of years before.

Some things are not reversible.

One day, with my bare feet sunk deep into the sand, while looking out at that great ocean from an African shore, I found myself tearful and drawn closer to a history I had not realized was still such a part of my recessed ancestral memory. All my childhood memories of fun, family times at the shore on the other side of the Atlantic and fishing with my grandfather, were pushed gently aside by waves of the memory of the trauma of the Middle Passage.

Prior to living outside the United States, I had always been a fish-fry kind of girl—usually catfish. My grandfather's favorite pastime was river and lake fishing. He and I would regularly go fishing, with hookworm, fly-fish, cooler, and home to cook our catch for that night's supper. I have always loved fried fish because it evokes that memory of the love.

One peaceful, star-filled night on a West African lagoon called the Baie de Sirènes, decades after the fishing trips with my grandfather, I had a memorable encounter with the fruits of the sea. At a thatch-roofed *maquis* on the water's edge, fish caught that day was charcoal grilled tableside under a powerfully close moon. It was served with tomato sauce and fresh vegetable condiments. The tastes amazed my palate and yet were familiar enough to take me back to my childhood memories with my grandfather, back to the other side of the Atlantic, holding a seashell to my ear and hearing the roar of the ocean's waves; leading me to explore and reappreciate fresh fish, simply prepared.

Whether on a Greek island, the Spanish seaside, southern France, or a West African shore, the best part of eating fish for me has always been the taste of the sea. The simpler, the better.

BROCHETTES WITH TOMATO SAUCE

Start to finish: 1 hour
Serves 4

Grouper fillet, 800g/1.75 pounds

12 overripe tomatoes
1 medium onion, chopped
2 garlic cloves, peeled and chopped
Fresh thyme
Lemon rind, grated
Scotch bonnet pepper

Maggi liquid seasoning
Bouillon cube
Tomato paste
1 teaspoon flour
Juniper berry, ground

Groundnut oil

Start with prepping the fish. Clean the fish and cut it into chunks to skewer. I like 2-inch chunks. Place in a bowl and season with fresh ground pepper, a crushed vegetable or poultry bouillon cube, a pinch of salt, a teaspoon of juniper berry, and a few splashes of Maggi. Mix well. This can be prepared ahead or closer to cooking. At a minimum, let the fish marinate for 30 minutes.

For the sauce, score the tomatoes and leave them in boiling water for a few minutes. Remove the tomatoes from the water. The skin should now be easy to peel off. Discard the skin.

Cut the tomatoes in half and remove as many of the seeds as you can.

In a saucepan, heat about 2 tablespoons of peanut oil. Lightly salt the oil. Add the chopped onion and let it brown. Then add the garlic and a few peppercorns, cook for a minute on medium heat, and then add the tomato flesh and 2 thyme branches with the leaves. Bring to a quick boil, cover and let simmer for 20 minutes. Loosely cover so the steam escapes. Stir occasionally.

In a small bowl, mix 2 tablespoons of tomato paste and 1 teaspoon of flour. Whisk in a little cold water, about ¼ cup, to make a smooth paste. Add this to the tomato sauce in the saucepan. Stir, then add the Scotch bonnet pepper and a splash of Maggi. Continue cooking, loosely covered, for 20 minutes. You want the sauce to thicken and not be runny. Salt to taste.

When ready to cook, 4 to 6 fish chunks per skewer is ideal. If using wooden skewers, you must soak them in water for 15 minutes before putting the fish on them. Once skewered, the fish can be cooked under a broiler for 3 to 5 minutes per side, or grilled in a skillet. Garnish with lemon zest and serve with quinoa or rice, and the tomato sauce.

Dishes with fish and rice were among my favorites of West African cuisines—peppery white rice with fish, tomato-soaked rice with fish, mouthwatering fried fish with rice or attieke. These dishes sound simple but are complex and so much depends on making sure the rice is cooked through, not too hard or too "wet." The dishes, layered with vegetables, are an art form. My recipe below is a humble taste.

FISH WITH RICE
Start to finish: 2 hours

Freshwater fish, 1 foot,
such as perch or carp

1 cup of fresh sorrel leaves
1 Scotch bonnet pepper
1 small white cabbage
1 green pepper, deseeded and quartered
3 carrots, peeled and cut in half
1 cup chopped parsley
Lemon
2 garlic cloves
1 onion, cut into 8 wedges

2 cups broken rice
Bay leaf
Maggi liquid seasoning
Peppercorns
Salt
Flour
Bouillon

Groundnut oil

Cut the cabbage in half and remove the hard stem and any brown leaves. Lightly steam the cabbage, carrots, and onion for about 15 minutes.

Clean the fish, which has been gutted. If you have sorrel, cook the leaves with a small green bonnet chili. It takes about 5 minutes for sorrel to steam. When done, remove the chili and keep aside. It will be used again in the rice. Strain the sorrel, let cool, then finely chop. Reserve this for the rice.

Cut the fish into 3-inch sections. Season with salt and pepper. Lightly coat in flour.

On medium heat, add ½ cup of oil to a large stockpot that has a lid. Season the oil with a healthy pinch of salt. Fry the fish in the oil on all sides. The fleshy ends should lightly brown. Remove from the oil and set in a baking dish. Place in the oven at about 160°C/325°F. The fish will finish cooking in the oven. Add the onions and green pepper to the oil. Lightly char the pepper skin. Add the bay leaf, a teaspoon of crushed peppercorns, garlic, and parsley. Sauté for 5 minutes. Add the cabbage, carrots, Scotch bonnet, and a few dashes of Maggi liquid seasoning. Salt to taste, and then a bit more salt. Cover and let the cabbage steam until cooked; so, for about ten more minutes.

Take a sieve spoon and remove the vegetables from the pot. Place the vegetables right on top of the fish in the dish in the oven. You want some of the vegetable flavors to mingle with the fish.

Add 2 cups of rice and a bouillon cube to the stockpot you removed the vegetables from. The bouillon can be vegetable, chicken, or fish. Stir well. Add the boiling water and the cooked sorrel. If this just covers the rice, that is sufficient. Cover the pot with a tea towel and then place a heavy lid on that, bring to a quick boil, and reduce to a very low heat. Let the rice cook like this for 20 minutes. The tea towel will absorb the steam. Once cooked, the rice will be savory with the taste of the fish and the vegetables and a pleasant tartness from the sorrel. To serve, place the rice on a large serving plate and arrange the fish and vegetables on top or around. Garnish with lemon wedges.

LEMON FRIED CHICKEN
Start to finish: 45–65 minutes
Serves 4–6

Season eight chicken pieces as desired. I prefer a basic coating of Ma Bell's, salt, ground black pepper, and garlic powder (1 teaspoon each) mixed with 2 tablespoons of flour. To ensure the seasoning adheres to the skin and meat, let the chicken sit with the coating for 10 minutes

Fry chicken in seasoned peanut oil. During the frying, sprinkle freshly squeezed lemon juice on the chicken. Do this several times. When turning the chicken, season the fried side with lemon juice and a bit of salt. Do be careful—some of the lemon juice will hit the oil and create an oil splash. Finish off in a warm oven for 20 minutes to ensure chicken is cooked through to the bone.

CHICKEN CURRY BROCHETTES

Start to finish: 1 hour, excluding marinating time
Serves 4

6 chicken thigh fillets, 3-inch cubed
2 boneless chicken breasts, 2-inch cubed

1 teaspoon freshly grated ginger
1 teaspoon freshly grated garlic
Freshly chopped coriander/cilantro (*optional*, to taste)

3 teaspoons curry powder
3 teaspoons garam masala
2 teaspoons turmeric powder
2 teaspoons cumin powder
1 teaspoon chili powder
bit of cinnamon stick
4 green cardamom pods

1 cup coconut milk (*optional*)
3 cups plain thick yogurt

In a glass bowl, mix all of the seasonings and yogurt (and coconut milk if desired). Add the chicken pieces and make sure they are well coated with the yogurt seasoning. Cover and leave in the fridge to marinate for at least 8 hours.

Remove the chicken from the fridge at least 30 minutes before cooking. Soak the skewers, if wood, in water for 10 minutes.

Skewer the chicken pieces; I like 6 to 8 pieces of meat per skewer. You can cook the chicken several ways, under the broiler, my preferred method, in a grill pan, or on a BBQ grill. To cook on the grill, you will need to oil the grill or use a nonstick grill pan. Broil or grill the chicken on both sides. Then leave in a warm oven for 15 minutes to ensure the meat is cooked through. Serve with salad and/or on basmati or pilau rice.

CHICKEN VERMICELLI
Start to finish: 90 minutes
Serves 6

2 small chickens

Juice of 1 lemon
3 medium onions, chopped
1 cup chopped curly parsley
1 cup finely diced carrot
1 cup green, pitted olives

Salt
Freshly ground pepper
Maggi liquid seasoning
1 level tablespoon mustard powder (Colman's)
1 onion-flavored bouillon cube or
level teaspoon onion powder

3 tablespoons of peanut oil

Chicken size varies from country to country. If in the United States, use one small chicken or perhaps two or three Cornish hens. Cut the chickens into eight pieces each. Wash, place in a bowl, pat dry, and then season with the lemon juice, salt, and pepper. The chicken can be seasoned the night before cooking.

Place the oil in a large skillet on medium-high heat. Season the oil with salt. Fry the chicken pieces in batches until the skin is brown. Set aside the chicken. In the same oil used to cook the chicken, brown the 3 onions, parsley, and carrot. Add a few drops of Maggi.

While that is sautéing, mix the mustard and onion powder in 1 to 1½ cups of water.

Once the onions begin to brown, add the mustard mix. Bring to a light boil, cover, and let simmer for 30 minutes. Place the chicken in an oven casserole dish that has a cover, add the onions, carrots, and sauce to the chicken and place in the oven to bake on low heat (180°C/350°F) for up to an hour. Add the olives a few minutes before serving to heat through. Serve over cooked vermicelli.

CHICKEN IN PEANUT SAUCE

While living in Africa, we enjoyed many varieties of peanut sauce. Some versions included varying combinations of lamb, guinea fowl, chicken, black-eyed peas, onion, okra, Scotch bonnet pepper, cabbage, carrot, white yams, spinach, and sorrel. And never black pepper, my sister-in-law would admonish!

My eldest sister-in-law had a wonderful kitchen. The food that came out of it was extraordinary. Layers of tradition, care, research, trials, and family secrets were evident in the succulence of each dish. Couscous properly steamed and rolled *à la main*, meat rubbed and marinated and cooked on the right type of wood charcoal. That is the only way you arrive at succulence. My children loved her food, and her table was a total pleasure for everyone. Her peanut sauce, *mafé*, sauce arachide, was the one thing I wanted to learn to do well because of my son's love for it. All peanut pastes are not created equal, and I learned the hard way that peanut butter sold in grocery stores does not hold up in an African-inspired peanut sauce. On moving back to France, I had to learn how to make this most favored dish of my son. *Dakatine* was the paste that I had to have; I was advised it was the best to use.

Whatever your combination of meats and vegetable, the base is what makes the sauce. Getting an acceptable base took me years of trial and error, tastings, and querying every cook's tips for what makes a good *mafé*. I persevered because my children loved it—even when too thick or too bland. One day of trial and a call to my sister-in-law unlocked my ability to make a tasty and smooth sauce—a good tomato sauce as a base starter. I do not believe that you can get a good smooth peanut sauce without this. On the surface, it is not obvious that peanut sauce has a tomato base, which is why this technique eluded me. I knew tomato paste was used, but the method tripped me up. Once I incorporated this base, I could take my sauce in any direction, soup-thin or spoon-sticking thick.

Prepare everything as if to make *sauce tomate* and then in a side dish mix some of the tomato sauce with peanut paste or what is commonly called peanut butter. NB: The peanut butter has to be smooth, made of peanuts (91–96 percent), palm oil, sea salt, preferably organic, and contain *no* added sugar. Basically, you want to get as close to pure peanuts as possible. You mix the butter and sauce until you have an easy-to-stir mixture. Then pour this mixture back into the tomato sauce. I have had this dish made with fowl, lamb, and beef respectively, and my favorite combination is with guinea fowl and white yam.

Start to finish: 2 hours
Serves 6

1 small chicken
½ guinea fowl

1 peeled medium-sized yellow onion
2 garlic cloves
1 large carrot
100 grams chopped fresh spinach
1 Scotch bonnet pepper if you want to add some heat
3–4 heaping tablespoons of groundnut butter

12 whole black peppercorns
1 bay leaf
1½ tubes tomato paste
Maggi liquid seasoning
Fish sauce (Thai anchovy sauce)
2 cups cooked black-eyed peas
2 chicken bouillon cubes

Place a large pan on low heat.

Clean and cut the chicken into eight pieces and the half guinea fowl into two. Place all of the fowl in the pan skin-side down and let sizzle for about 15 minutes. Turn the pieces of chicken over midway. The skin should not shred or pull when you go to turn it. If it does, let it cook until you can easily turn it over.

Season with salt, add the peppercorns, peeled whole onion, bay leaf, peeled garlic cloves, 2 tablespoons of Maggi, and 1 tablespoon of fish sauce.

Add 1 tube of tomato paste and gently stir the poultry around.

Add the water. Bring to a boil, cover, and simmer for 30 minutes.

Remove the chicken, peppercorns, and bay leaf from the sauce to a baking dish. Take a handheld mixer and pulverize *only* the onion and garlic in the sauce.

Place the peanut butter in a large bowl. Whisk in approximately 3 cups of tomato sauce, a cup at a time.

To the main tomato sauce, add 2 chicken bouillon cubes, ½ tube of tomato paste, and a sprinkle of salt.

Pour the peanut tomato mix back into the pot with the main sauce. (*Optional*: add the whole Scotch bonnet pepper to the sauce.) Stir well on medium heat and leave to simmer for 30 minutes.

Add the spinach and carrot and continue simmering for 30 minutes. Strain and rinse the black-eyed peas.

Place the fowl pieces back in the pot, pouring the rinsed black-eyed peas on top, and simmer for another 30 minutes; heat through, stir occasionally, and essentially the sauce is finished. Carefully remove the Scotch bonnet pepper to avoid crushing.

Present the fowl on a plate and the sauce in a bowl. This dish is eaten with steamed white rice. Because it is heavy and complete, an appetizer is not recommended.

Variations: Cubes of white yam can also be added to the sauce, as can chopped or whole okra. Place the chopped okra in a sieve and rinse well to remove the gelatin. Do not combine okra and spinach in the same sauce.

OVEN YASSA

In this dish from Senegal, marinated chicken is traditionally cooked over charcoal. I have never been able to handle cooking on charcoal or barbecuing, so I have substituted oven broiling for barbecuing and find this dish just as satisfying. This dish requires marinating one (preferably) free-range corn-fed chicken for at least 8 hours.

Start to finish: 2 hours
Serves 6

1 chicken

6 yellow onions
2 garlic cloves, crushed
Juice of 3 lemons
Fresh thyme

Black peppercorns
Ground black pepper
2 tablespoons red wine vinegar
1 heaping teaspoon Dijon or white wine mustard
Bay leaf
1 chicken bouillon cube

Groundnut oil

You will need an airtight container large enough to hold all of the chicken parts laid out flat. Butterfly or cut the chicken into two sections. Wash and pierce the skin and flesh with a sharp knife in several places so that the marinade will penetrate.

Peel and slice 6 onions paper thin. Wear eye goggles if onions make you cry.

Add the vinegar, mustard, crushed bouillon cube, bay leaf, and garlic to the lemon juice. Whisk together. This is the marinade for the chicken. Score the chicken in several places. Season the chicken on both sides with salt, pepper, and thyme. Use about 1 teaspoon of thyme per half chicken. Liberally season the chicken with ground black pepper.

Place half of the sliced onions on the bottom of the airtight container; season with salt and pepper. Place the chicken skin-side down on top of the onions. Pierce the chicken with the knife again. Spread the remaining onions on top of the chicken. Salt the onions, about a teaspoon. The salt will help draw the juice out of the onions to enhance the marinade.

Pour the lemon marinade over the chicken and onions. Seal the container and shake the mixture around a bit. Place in the fridge. After 4 hours or overnight resting, shake the container around again.

When ready to cook, preheat the oven to 220°C/425°F. Remove the chicken from the fridge and let stand for 20 minutes. Place the chicken and onions in a baking dish, breast-side up if butterflied. Bake in the oven at a high temperature for 20 minutes. After 20 minutes, add 2 cups of water to the pan and reduce the heat to 200°C/400°F. Leave to bake for 1 hour.

Then turn the oven off and leave the chicken in the oven a further 20 minutes. The chicken should have a brown glaze when done. Place the chicken on a plate to serve with steamed white rice, preferably Thai jasmine rice.

Put the onion sauce in a sauce dish or small bowl to serve with the dish. The sauce is very concentrated, so use sparingly.

For a more calorie-intensive approach, which I prefer, rather than bake the onions in the oven with the chicken, you can fry the onions in 4 or 5 tablespoons of peanut oil while the chicken is baking. For the last 20 minutes, you remove the chicken from the oven and add it to the fried onions along with its juices. Mix well, cover, and let simmer for 15 minutes.

ATTIECHICKEN

This braised chicken with a vinegary shredded vegetable condiment was loved by my youngest son. Not able to pronounce attieké, the manioc couscous popular in West Africa, and chicken, he melded the two into "attiechicken."

Start to finish: 30 minutes, excluding time to grill meat
Serves 4

                                                              1 chicken

    1 large onion
    1 green bell pepper
    4 plum tomatoes
    Fresh thyme
    Chili pepper (*optional*)

                                            Maggi liquid seasoning
                               Apple cider or red wine vinegar
    Peanut oil

Generously season chicken pieces to taste with salt, pepper, and Maggi before grilling. This can be done in advance to let the seasoning penetrate the meat.

Condiment for grilled or barbecued chicken or fish.
Slice one large onion and 1 green bell pepper paper thin. Slice 4 plum tomatoes equally fine and let the seeds run out. Place all in a bowl and season with 2 to 4 tablespoons of peanut oil, 2 tablespoons of vinegar (apple cider or red wine), 1 teaspoon of fresh thyme, salt, and fresh ground pepper to taste. Diced hot pepper as well as a splash of Maggi can also be added.

Use this vegetable condiment to garnish the chicken once grilled. Make enough to have extra on the side.

Serve with couscous, quinoa, or attieké.

KEDJENOU—GAME STEW

Start to finish: 90 minutes
Serves 2–4

1 guinea fowl

1 tablespoon freshly grated ginger
½ zucchini, grated
2 yellow onions, grated
1 medium carrot, diced
1 cup chopped parsley
Juice of ½ lemon
1 Scotch bonnet pepper
Chopped tomato (canned or 8 fresh)
Thyme

Maggi liquid seasoning

Cut the fowl into eight pieces and place all of the ingredients into a pot or pressure cooker. I do not use pressure cookers and prefer a heavy-lidded pot to trap the steam. Once the pot lid is on, I often place a smaller, heavy pan on top to really seal the pot closed. Mix the ingredients well. On a medium-high heat, cook the fowl for about 10 minutes. Reduce to low, tightly cover the pot and cook for approximately 1 hour (or if using a pressure cooker, according to its instructions). Serve over rice or with manioc couscous.

CASABLANCA COUSCOUS

While living in West Africa, I had the good fortune and occasion to visit Morocco, where I enjoyed many a homemade meal, unlike anything on offer in a restaurant.

This almost ceremonial dish brings back all my memories of Morocco and has one of the things I found most special about Moroccan cuisine, the use of orange flower water. I enjoyed this dish at a home in Casablanca during a visit, but I only attempted to make it many years later. It had a lasting impression as it was served on a large, round, ornately hammered brass serving plate, which the guests sat around to communally enjoy. This recipe allows for leftover lamb to make a hearty Moroccan lamb soup called *harira*, my version.

Start to finish: half a day
Serves 8–10

1 leg of lamb or boneless lamb shoulder, seasoned many hours or the night before

Coriander/cilantro, 1½ cups chopped
Curly parsley, 1½ cups chopped
Fresh mint leaves, ¼ cup chopped
2 garlic cloves
8–10 plum tomatoes
1 small turnip,
1 large zucchini
Fresh thyme
1 large eggplant
4 carrots
1 medium brown onion, chopped

2 cups cooked chickpeas
Cumin

Thyme
Bay leaf
Chili powder
Garlic powder
Saffron

Butter
Olive oil

Garnish/Relish
For the unforgettable garnish, served alongside the couscous:

4 small onions, sliced paper thin
Sultanas that are not black or golden raisins, but the
brown ones in between
Honey, preferably orange blossom
Orange blossom water
Cinnamon sticks

Unwrap the meat and clean it; I have half a shoulder and half a boneless leg (without the shank).

Prepare a dry rub for the lamb. In a bowl, mix together 3 tablespoons of cumin, 2 teaspoons of thyme, 1 crushed large bay leaf, 1 teaspoon chili powder, 2 teaspoons of garlic powder, 3 teaspoons of salt, and a dash of pepper. The amount of salt and chili powder can be adjusted to taste. Clean and pierce the meat all over with a sharp knife. Massage the meat with the dry rub. I use gloves for rubbing the meat. This can marinate for 4 hours or overnight in the refrigerator. A few hours before preparing the couscous, remove the lamb from the cold and let it rest to come to room temperature.

For the sauce, take a tall stockpot. Gather the vegetables, herbs, oil, and seasoning.

Cut the eggplant into quarters, place in a colander, and salt the white flesh. Let sit for 20 minutes. The salt will draw out the bitter juices from the eggplant.

Melt 8 tablespoons of butter in the pot on medium heat. Start with the onions, a sprig of fresh thyme, and a bay leaf; sauté them in the butter. When the onions start to brown, add the herbs (parsley, cilantro, mint). Also, add a tablespoon of olive oil, if you like. Essentially, I am going to make a big broth. Season the herbs with salt, about 2 level teaspoons, and fresh ground pepper. Pepper is optional. Sometimes I prefer whole peppercorns to ground pepper. Continue cooking on medium for about 5 minutes and then add 8 to 10 chopped tomatoes and the garlic cloves. Sauté this mixture for about 10 minutes. Add a liter and a half of water to the pot along with three to five saffron threads. Bring to a mild boil and reduce the heat to a simmer. Preheat the oven to 220°C/425°F.

Anecdotally, on this occasion, I did not prepare the meat ahead. I chopped the onion on my chopping glass, set it aside, and afterward also seasoned the meat on the same glass so that it absorbed some of the onion juice as well. I then chopped the herbs on the glass to take up some of the meat seasoning.

Let the broth simmer for an hour.

Place the meat in a roasting pan, pour a cup of water in the pan, and roast on high for 20 minutes. After 20 minutes, reduce the oven temperature to 170°C/350°F and let slow roast for an hour and 10 minutes.

Once the meat is in the oven, turn back to the stockpot and add a large carrot cut into four pieces, the turnip, and a zucchini cut into four pieces. Thirty minutes in, add the rinsed eggplant. Simmer for another hour.

Garnish preparation:

Let 1 cup of sultanas sit in a bowl of hot water to plump.

Thinly slice four small onions on the round. Sauté in 100g/6 tablespoons of butter on a medium heat with a sliver of cinnamon stick. Cover and let simmer until the onions are translucent. Then add two threads of saffron to the onions.

When the onions are very soft, strain the raisins and add to the onions and let this simmer covered for 40 minutes. Then add some honey, about ⅓ of a cup. The final touch when ready to serve is to add a bit of orange flower water.

Do check the meat while slow roasting, basting occasionally. When the meat is done, remove it from the oven. Let rest. Take the juices from the baking pan and add to the vegetable stock.

Prepare the couscous according to the cooking instructions. Serve with the lamb, sultana relish, and broth.

NOT QUITE CHICKEN GUMBO

Growing up allergic to shellfish, I could only envy family when they were enjoying gumbo over steamed rice. In West Africa, gumbo is the name of the okra vegetable, and is equally and differently enjoyed in sauces. The sauces I tasted in national dishes were usually thicker from the gelatinous liquid of the okra, and quite strong in flavor; one was also stewed with a bitter eggplant-like vegetable. This recipe is made without the traditional American roux, crab claws, and andouille sausage, which is why it is not quite gumbo.

Start to finish: 2 hours
Serves 4–6

whole chicken cut into 8 pieces,

12 okra
2 green jalapeno peppers, deseeded and diced
1 onion, finely diced
2 cloves garlic, finely chopped
1 carrot, finely diced
Bouquet of curly parsley, finely chopped
2 fresh thyme sprigs

Fish sauce
Maggi liquid seasoning
Apple cider vinegar
12 whole peppercorns
Tube of tomato paste or 8 oz chopped tomatoes
1 bay leaf

Peanut oil

Take a deep stockpot and place it on medium heat. Thinly slice the okra. I put it in a colander and run it under hot water to rinse out as much of the gelatinous interior as possible. Place 1 tablespoon of oil in the pot. The oil is optional. Salt the oil. Add all of the vegetables and the bay leaf. Brown the vegetables for ten minutes, then add a tablespoon of vinegar and fish sauce, and 2 or 3 tablespoons of Maggi. Stir well. Cover with a tight lid, and let simmer for 20 minutes.

After 20 minutes, add a tube of tomato paste and the water. Stir well; continue simmering. Lightly coat the chicken with flour. Fry the chicken pieces in peanut oil seasoned with salt. When turning, season with salt and fresh ground pepper. Only fry the chicken to brown the skin; the meat will finish cooking in the sauce. Place the chicken pieces in the pot with the okra/gumbo. Mix the chicken and vegetable sauce well. Let simmer until the chicken is cooked through.

QUICK GUMBO
Start to finish: 90 minutes
Serves 4

800g/1½ lb. of meat

12 okra, coarsely chopped
1 onion, diced
1 green pepper, diced
½ cup of chopped curly parsley
2 green chilis, diced
1 large garlic clove, finely chopped
2–3 sprigs fresh thyme
Carrot, chopped

1 can chopped tomatoes
Maggi liquid seasoning
Liquid smoke
8 peppercorns

4 tablespoons peanut oil,

Chop all of the vegetables. Cut the meat into at least eight chunks. Heat the peanut oil in a large saucepan with a cover. Salt the oil. Add the peppercorns, garlic, onion, and meat. Brown the meat. Add a dash of liquid smoke and Maggi— about a tablespoon of each. Add the remaining ingredients. Cover and reduce to simmer. Let simmer for an hour on very low heat.

LAMB OR MUTTON RAGU WITH LENTILS

Start to finish: 2–3 hours slow cooking
Serves 6–8

2-pound/1-kilogram lamb leg

2 large onions, finely chopped
1 cup curly parsley
4 garlic cloves, peeled
2 celery stalks, finely diced
3 carrots, scrubbed clean and cut into large pieces
5 potatoes, peeled and cut into quarters

Level teaspoon black ground pepper
2 level teaspoons salt
1 tablespoon Dijon mustard
3 teaspoons herbs de Provence
1 large bay leaf
2 cups cooked lentils

4 tablespoons olive oil

Wash the lamb and cut into large chunks. Place in a bowl and season with 1 teaspoon of ground black pepper, 2 teaspoons of salt, the mustard, the herbes de Provence, and the olive oil. Cover and place in the refrigerator to marinate. This can be done overnight or for 20 minutes.

Remove the meat from the refrigerator 1 hour prior to cooking. When ready to prepare the meat, dry sauté the vegetables for about 10 minutes and season with salt, pepper, and one bay leaf. Add the lamb and increase the temperature. Brown the lamb pieces. Reduce temperature, cover and let simmer for 45 minutes. Then stir and add the carrots and potatoes. Let simmer until the potatoes are almost tender. Then add 2 cups of cooked lentils. Canned lentils are fine. You may need to add up to 1 cup of water. Stir well and let simmer for 20 minutes.

BEEF RIBS IN TOMATO SAUCE
Start to finish: 5 hours slow cooking
Serves 6–8

6 beef short ribs

1 medium yellow onion, peeled and left whole
2 carrots scrubbed clean
¼ wedge of a small white cabbage
3 garlic cloves
A fistful of chopped curly parsley

1 tablespoon Maggi liquid seasoning
Peppercorns
Bay leaf
Thai fish sauce (about 2 tablespoons)
Red chili paste (not sweet) or
1 Scotch bonnet pepper
Red wine vinegar (about 1 cup)
1½ tubes tomato paste (about 2 cups)

Take a large casserole with a tight lid.

Clean the ribs and place them in the pot along with the whole peeled onion, garlic cloves, bay leaf, salt, peppercorns, red wine vinegar and the water. Bring to a boil and then reduce the heat and let simmer for 3 hours.

When done, the meat will easily slide off the bones. Remove the meat and bones from the broth—carefully. You may have to skim a bit of scum out of the edges of the pan; this is normal.

Now whisk or stir the tomato paste, fish sauce, and Maggi into the broth. Add the chopped parsley, hot pepper, carrots, and cabbage to the broth.

Bring to a brisk bubble then reduce heat and let simmer for 1 hour.

Add the beef portions without the bone back to the sauce. Stir in and simmer uncovered until sauce is sticking to the meat but still saucy enough to be spooned over rice.

DIRTY RICE

Rice is resplendent in cooking in West Africa. It was the family's spoonful of sugar, a mainstay that helped navigate the ups and downs of life wherever we found ourselves. A little of southern American and West African flavors found their way into this version of dirty rice.

Start to finish: 1 hour
Serves 4

500g/1 lb. of ground veal

1 yellow onion, finely diced
1 small red pepper, finely diced
1 small green pepper, finely diced
1 cup chopped parsley
4 cups chopped okra

Garlic powder
Black peppercorns
Chili flakes
Fish sauce
Maggi liquid seasoning
1 chicken stock cube
Bay leaf
2½ cups of long grain, or Thai jasmine rice

Peanut oil

Merguez sausage can replace the veal if preferred. If using merguez, do not add the chili flakes or red pepper.

Heat, on low, about ¼ cup of oil in a large saucepan that has a tight-fitting lid. Season the oil with salt.

I always rinse the okra before cooking by placing it in a large fine-mesh sieve and then running under hot water to remove some of the gelatinous fluid. There will be a lot of runoff.

Once the okra is rinsed and ready to go, increase the heat of the pan to medium. Let the pan get hot but not so hot that the oil burns. Add all of the vegetables and herbs to the pan along with a teaspoon of garlic powder, 8 to 10 peppercorns, the bay leaf, and the chicken stock cube. (Fresh crushed garlic can be used if powder is not readily available. I would use 2 large cloves). Stir well. Cover with a tight lid and let cook for 20 minutes on low heat. Stir well and increase the heat to medium. Once sizzling, add 1 tablespoon of fish sauce and 2 tablespoons of Maggi.

Stir in the veal so that it breaks up into mince. Add 1 teaspoon chili flakes. Salt to taste, at least 1 teaspoon for good measure. Let cook for ten minutes or so, uncovered.

Stir the uncooked rice into the mixture. You can optionally add more salt. Add just enough hot water to cover the rice. Bring to a boil, immediately reduce to a simmer, cover the pan with a tight lid, and let cook for 20 minutes—the time for the rice to cook through. Stir the rice to make sure all of the grains are cooked. Enjoy with a large garden salad with a creamy dressing.

Dessert

TROPICAL FRUIT SALAD

My eldest's first solid food must have been fresh mango. I remember coming home one day to find him sitting on the kitchen counter, a happy, sticky mango mess. The babysitter was helping him enjoy sucking the fruit flesh off the mango seed—so much better than a lollipop. For non-bakers, fruit is as reliable a dessert as the ice cream sundae.

Serves 4–6

Flesh of 2 ripe mangos, diced
1 cup chopped pineapple
1 or 2 ripe bananas, thinly sliced
Flesh of 1 large ripe papaya
Juice of 1 lime
6 passion fruit
Fresh mint, chopped *(optional)*

Cut the papaya into small teaspoon-size chunks, place in a glass bowl, and cover with the lime juice. Add the mango, pineapple, bananas as desired, and the flesh and juice of the passion fruit. Mix well, let marinate in its juices. When ready to serve, garnish with chopped fresh mint leaves if desired.

Variation: Two cups of diced melon (honeydew) can also be added.

Part 4

THE UNITED KINGDOM

STIRRING THE POT

Due to political circumstances that culminated in a coup d'etat, we left Africa and our life briefly segued back to France before a decision was made to pursue opportunities in the Anglo-Saxon world. Our sights turned to England. By the time I arrived in England, family in tow, my cooking had evolved with American, French, and West and North African flavors. Those learned cooking styles somehow comfortably began to find each other and to blossom. My kitchen practices came to reflect what I took as the best of my accumulated experiences, my keys to success in the kitchen.

My family and I arrived in England amid a period of outbreaks among livestock of mad cow and foot-and-mouth diseases. The food situation seemed perilous. Moving from France, just across the channel, a stone's throw it seemed, I thought, one cannot live in England without thinking about French food.

In the early days, I would make regular trips back to France to stock up on food items, some of which I would freeze. While I relied on exploring the local markets to find my footing and the life and pulse of places on my initial arrivals in

Europe and Africa, England was slightly different. There were not as many local outdoor markets as in Paris. And they tended to lean toward offering a variety of already "home" prepared dishes. The grocery stores became the mainstay for food, and they were quite good. For bread, cheeses, and meats, I sought out specialist shops and was not disappointed, establishing excellent relations with my suppliers just as I had everywhere else.

As we grew into our new home and abodes, I had the opportunity to design my own kitchen HQ, and establish my own rules for running a family kitchen. Before England, I was heavily replicating others' good practices as I learned. Running a kitchen is a learning process and, while trial and error are normal, I believe there are some basics. A few from my personal learning curve are set out here.

The key to kitting out your kitchen, and making a foundation for good food, begins with your local knowledge of what is on offer to stock your kitchen.

Before thinking about undertaking cooking, it is worth thinking about how you like to work with food and in the kitchen. For example, I like to be alone when I am cooking. That moment of solitude harkens back to memories of my grandmothers working their magic and appearing out of a room with a feast. There was always an element of surprise. My maternal grandmother religiously believed in preparing the entire day's meals early in the morning, before everyone in the house was up. Her secrets were safe! Another influence on my food philosophy was linked to a rebellion against cooking, as it was for my mother and grandmothers. Or, perhaps the rebellion was a reverse intuitive defense to help me absorb all of the new-to-me cooking techniques I had to learn as I embraced my life abroad.

"Do two cooks truly spoil a broth?" The women in my family strongly believed, "Yes." Even when busy with a hectic schedule and running around and managing a lot of commitments, I still wanted to have that nice idyllic family meal at the end of the day. I was often far from home, calling my children as they got older with instructions to "turn on the oven," "stir that," "turn the temperature down," "boil the water," "chop." So, actually, a broth can have input from more than one cook and come out fine, delicious even. When everyone has done what they needed to do in the day and can still sit down together and enjoy a meal on time because someone else helped you along the way, actually, two cooks can sometimes make the broth taste better.

Having moved around so much, I took a step back to assess what I had learned from all those cooks and suppliers and what I would use. While in Africa, I learned about seasoning meat and seasoning a pan. In Europe, I discovered the value of a cookbook. Every cook needs one cookbook that forms their foundation, serves as their bible, complements their nature and helps them develop their *hand*, their signature taste. In my experience in Africa, when you had a delicious meal, really good, it was stated, with deference, that the cook has a "good hand." Conversely, it was often expressed with compassion after a not-so-good meal that the hosts made an exemplary effort, code for they don't have a "hand." One knew the homes where a meal would lack the alchemy of the joy of flavors.

And from my early Paris days as a novice home chef, my learning and meal assessment became dictated by the question, "*Is* a clean kitchen the sign of a good cook?" Was the measure of the goodness of my meals, each recipe attempted, directly linked to how neat the kitchen was after the preparation? To debate, certainly. But in my experience, yes, it is. Since that debut couples' dinner in Paris, whenever I visit someone's home for a meal, I always note the state of the kitchen that has put forth the fare to come.

From a solid foundation, one can build a repertoire with other cookbooks, recipes, and influences, such as family home-cooking traditions.

Food for Thought

Markets, habits, tools
Savvy, organization
Well-being assured

Give some thought to where you want your equipment placed. My ideal kitchen would have the stovetop next to the sink and the refrigerator next to the largest worktop.

To inform your shopping habits, think about the following: Do you like everything precut, frozen? Can you live with delivery? Is organic important? How do you feel about guts? Do they make you uncomfortable?

I cook by smell and not by taste. In fact, I have a real dislike of tasting food during its preparation. Figure out how you know when a dish is just right.

When preparing food, I usually wear vinyl gloves to protect my skin, so my hands don't smell of garlic, etc. Some vegetables are great for the skin, so gloves off when this is the case; relish the tactile pleasure of potatoes, avocados, oil from lemon skin, rosemary, thyme, and mint.

When cutting or peeling vegetables, do it over a disposable grocery bag. Peel the potatoes right into the bag or onto a board to make them easy to dump into the compost. This makes for easy cleanup. You can also cut the ends off some veggies while they are in their bag.

When you are ready to cook, it pays to thoroughly read the recipe before you start cooking.

Prep time includes prepping, not sourcing, of ingredients and cooking time from start to finish.

Stainless steel pans are preferable to Teflon-coated pans. Teflon just does not brown the food to my liking.

Keep a good pair of scissors for food, not for anything else.

Courtesy must be taught. After emptying the dishwasher, refill the soap compartment. It is the kitchen equivalent of leaving the toilet seat down.

Sharpen a knife before putting it back in the knife block.

Equipment

Six-inch ruler—metric and imperial
1-cup measure/155g
Blowtorch
Corkscrew
Digital food scale
Glass work surface/cutting board
Good graters—handheld and containerized
Good knife
Handheld fine sieve
Plastic serrated knife for cutting vegetables
Salad spinner
Standing bowl colander
Vegetable peeler (They're not just for peeling skin off vegetables; they also make useful vegetable ribbons for salads.)
Vinyl, latex-free, skin-like gloves

Cupboard

Baking powder
Baking soda (Sodium bicarbonate)

Canned beans
Chipotle powder
Colman's mustard powder
Cornstarch
Cumin powder
Fish sauce
Lemon zest
Liquid smoke
Ma Bell's poultry seasoning
Maggi liquid seasoning
Nutritional yeast
Oils
Olive oil
Peanut oil (It does not burn and adds a sweet aroma.)
Sunflower and Safflower oil
Toasted sesame oil
Pomi sieved tomatoes
Powdered coconut milk (It keeps well and is great when you don't have canned coconut milk handy or do not need an entire can.)
Salted butter
Sea salt
Sesame oil
Sriracha
Thai jasmine rice
Vinegars! Cannot have enough.
Vogel Herbamare (herb-infused sea salt)

Salads—Starters—Soups

BB'S CHESTNUT SOUP

Chestnuts mean autumn, chilly sunny days with blue skies, sweaters, and cold cheeks, kicking leaves in the park. Christmas is around the corner. When my sons were little, I felt soup was integral to their growth and happiness. Soup, an all-around, multipurpose, pleasurable food: a healthy starter, a needed filler, an easy elegance booster for guests, an economical and leftover-friendly main course, and, sometimes, a remedy or nurse. Soup can just feel like a warm hug. Not many dishes do fill so many roles. My eldest son loved chestnuts, hence this recipe for him to warm autumn and winter evenings.

Start to finish: 90 minutes
Serves 4–6

1 large leek
1 Jerusalem artichoke
1 large celery stalk
2½ to 3 cups cooked chestnuts

Chicken stock cube
Unsalted butter

Chop the cleaned leek, artichoke, and celery and sauté in a deep pan in about 2 tablespoons of unsalted quality butter for 5 minutes. Season with salt. The leeks should begin to brown. Then add the chestnuts and stir well. Add the water and the cube of chicken stock. Bring to a boil and then leave to simmer for an hour. Add salt as desired and puree the mixture. Taste for salt and adjust seasoning. At this time, you may need to add some hot water, not more than a cup, to adjust the soup's thickness. Stir in a teaspoon of crème fraîche.

ZUCCHINI SOUP

Served cold in summer or warm in autumn. Some minced cucumber is a perfect garnish for the cold version of this soup, and miniature croutons serve as the same for the warm version.

Start to finish: 40 minutes
Serves 6

  3 zucchini
  3 fresh mint leaves
  2 small leeks

                          Fresh ground pepper
                          1 vegetable stock cube
                          1 chicken stock cube

  2 tablespoons salted butter
  1 tablespoons crème fraîche

Sauté the zucchini and leeks in the butter to brown the leeks. Add the rest of the ingredients. Let cook, covered, on medium heat for 30 minutes.

GREEN SOUP

This soup is made with the husks left over from spiralized zucchini.

Start to finish: 40 minutes
Serves 4

    1 leek
    5 zucchini husks and bits
    200g baby spinach
    1 large peeled and deseeded cucumber

                        1 vegetable stock bouillon cube
                                1 liter filtered water

    Olive oil *(optional)*

Dry sauté the vegetables and stock cube in a large saucepan on medium heat for 5 minutes. The leek should begin to brown and dry on the edges. Add the filtered water to the vegetables. Bring to a boil, then reduce and let simmer for half an hour. Blend the ingredients with a hand blender. A drizzle of olive oil can be added if desired.

WATERCRESS SOUP
Start to finish: 60 minutes
Serves 6–8

2 bunches clean organic watercress
1 small carrot
1 small leek, chopped
1 medium white potato, peeled and chopped

Fresh ground black pepper
Chicken or vegetable stock

Butter (*optional*)
1 tablespoon crème fraîche (*optional*)

Chop the leek, carrot, and potato and place in a pan on medium heat. This can be dry sautéed or browned with some salted butter. I prefer it without butter.

Clean the cress and add to the saucepan. This will quickly wilt.

Season with fresh ground pepper and 1 chicken stock cube.

Add the water to the vegetables, bring to a boil, and then reduce heat and let simmer for as long as you like (40 minutes is sufficient).

When ready to serve, blend the soup with a hand mixer right in the pot. Add about 3 pinches of salt and stir. Let simmer for 5 more minutes if you have added a tablespoon of crème fraîche.

Variation: Spinach and celery can also be added to this to make a tasty green soup.

PEA AND CRESS SOUP

Start to finish: 30 minutes
Delicious and simply one of the easiest soups to make.

Chop one large leek and sauté in 2 tablespoons of unsalted French butter. Add at least 3 cups of frozen peas and two large handfuls of fresh watercress. Stir and season with a pinch of salt and pepper. Add a vegetable bouillon cube and cover with 6–8 cups of water. Bring to a boil and simmer for 40 minutes. Blend with a handheld blender. Serve with crusty bread.

This soup can also be garnished with chopped fresh mint, chopped ham, or Parmesan croutons.

SOUP SMORGASBORD

This recipe is great for large groups. Everyone can make his or her own soup. For the vegetables, the quantity will depend on the number of guests. A bowl of soup can take 2 tablespoons of roasted vegetable toppings.

Start to finish: 90 minutes

Base of Potato Leek soup

Diced ham

Asparagus
Mushrooms
Carrots
Garlic
Parsley

Herbamare
Cumin powder

Olive oil
Butter *(optional)*

Vegetable chip toppings:

Thinly slice the carrots and asparagus on the diagonal, dice the mushrooms, and season as desired before roasting to dry into "chips." Roast the carrots, asparagus, and mushrooms separately with the following seasonings:

Asparagus (season with white pepper and olive oil)

Mushrooms (season with garlic and parsley)

Carrots (season with salt and cumin powder)

Roasting can be done at 200°C/400°F. Stir the vegetables half-way through cooking.

Sauté the diced ham in a tablespoon of butter.

Present each topping in a bowl, serve the soup base, and each person can add toppings as they desire.

QUINOA SALAD

This salad is delicious on its own, with grilled meat, vegetables, or my favorite, fried fish. It also adds variety to a mezze selection.

Start to finish: 30 minutes
Serves 8–10

1½ cups uncooked quinoa
1 cup uncooked bulgur wheat

2 spring onions, thinly sliced
A generous handful of arugula leaves
1 bunch watercress
1½ cups cherry tomatoes, deseeded and coarsely chopped
Juice of one lemon

1 tablespoon balsamic vinegar
Herbamare

½ to ¾ cup olive oil

This is the only way I will eat quinoa. The bulgur wheat is optional but adds bulk to absorb the vegetable dressing.

Boil the quinoa and bulgur wheat as per the cooking instructions, and let cool.

While the grains are cooking, wash the cress, stems and all, and the arugula, and place in a blender with the olive oil, the lemon juice, balsamic vinegar, and a pinch of sea salt, and blend. The consistency should coat a spoon. If too thick, add more olive oil. Once the grains are cool, place them in a glass bowl, season with a bit of Herbamare, and mix the two grains. Add the scallions, tomatoes, and dressing. Mix well.

Variation: The salad can be topped with roasted almond slivers or pistachios. To completely change the flavor, after mixing the watercress dressing with the quinoa, add toasted pistachio and roasted cherry tomatoes and top with fried onions.

ARTICHOKE AND CLEMENTINE SALAD

8–10 artichokes in olive oil
225–300g/2 cups steamed string beans
1 diced yellow pepper
2 diced and deseeded tomatoes
Wedges of 3 clementines
Bibb or Baby Gem lettuce

Wash the lettuce. Coarsely pull apart. I prefer the smaller Baby Gem leaves for this salad. On a chopping board, slice the artichokes lengthwise into thirds. Place them in a large bowl where you can toss all of the ingredients together. Cut the tips off the string beans and discard/compost the tips. Cut the string beans in half and toss with the artichokes. Add the remaining vegetables and clementine wedges and toss. Arrange the lettuce leaves on a plate and place the vegetables on top.

TEX-MEX

2 ripe avocados
Apple cider vinegar
Herbamere
Freshly ground pepper
Olive oil
165g or ¾ cup corn
Bunch (about a cup) chopped cilantro
1 large beefsteak tomato, cut into large dice

Whisk together 2 tablespoons of apple cider vinegar, Herbamare, and freshly ground pepper and then whisk in a steady stream of ½ cup of olive oil. Toss the corn, cilantro, and tomato together. Dress the tossed vegetables.

To prepare the avocado, remove the skin and slice in half lengthwise. Remove the pit. Discard the skin and pit. You can choose to dice the avocado flesh and toss with the other vegetables, or thinly slice the avocado lengthwise and arrange on a plate to then cover with the corn mixture once dressed.

TEX-MEX II

Clean, deseed, and chop 10 vine-ripe tomatoes

Clean lettuce of choice and arrange leaves on a plate. Make eight small piles of tomato on the lettuce. Sprinkle each pile with a generous pinch of dried thyme leaves. You can also use fresh thyme leaves. Season with Herbamare and fresh ground pepper. Pour ½ teaspoon of balsamic vinegar and a teaspoon of olive oil over each pile. This is a nice refreshing salad to serve with spicy, non-tomato-based enchiladas.

ASPARAGUS, GREEN BEAN, AND WALNUT SALAD

200g/2 cups each of asparagus and string beans. Steam the string beans. Cut the asparagus into halves and steam them as well. When done, lightly coat the drained vegetables with mustard vinaigrette. When ready to serve, top with hand-crushed walnut pieces.

FETA SALAD

1 cup pitted kalamata or black olives
180–200g/2 cups organic feta cheese
1 cup black seedless grapes, halved
⅛ or ¼ red onion, thinly sliced
Olive oil, as desired
Fresh ground pepper
Red bell pepper, halved and thinly sliced
2 cups/300g of diced cucumber
Slicing tomatoes *(optional)*

Break up the cheese in a large bowl. The olives can be chopped or halved, as you like. Similarly, the cucumber can be with or without the skin—just deseed. Mix all of the ingredients with the cheese. Serve on slices of tomatoes or alone.

AVO-BLUE WITH A BIBB

Diced flesh of one small, ripe avocado. About a tablespoon of crumbled blue cheese from Auvergne. Stir the two together. Season with a pinch of salt, fresh ground pepper, mustard vinaigrette, and a tablespoon of apple cider vinegar. Place the mixture in a serving dish. Place cleaned and separated Bibb leaves on top of the mixture. Toss when ready to serve.

ROMAINE AND RADISH WITH HONEY MUSTARD DRESSING

Cut the romaine in half lengthwise, and rinse clean. They can be brushed with olive oil and slightly charred in a grill pan or under a broiler or served plain. Arrange on a plate and top with thinly sliced radishes. Dress with honey-mustard dressing.

SHAVINGS

Mix ultra-thinly shaved asparagus, celery, fennel, zucchini, leeks or any combination. The vegetables can be very lightly steamed, as well, if preferred, but not to lose their firmness. Over low heat, pour ½ cup of olive oil in a small saucepan and add at least ½ cup of anchovies. Whisk until the anchovies are smooth, adding small drizzles of olive oil if needed, and whisk in ⅓ cup of lemon juice to create an emulsion. Dress the vegetables with the anchovy dressing.

TARRAGON SALAD

Dress edible flowers, baby green leaves, and fresh tarragon leaves with a light balsamic vinaigrette.

ZUCCHINI, FENNEL, AND KRAUT

Spiralize a zucchini. Thinly slice a fennel bulb. Place the zucchini spirals in a large bowl and further cut through the spirals so you don't have whole spirals. Add the fennel and 2 heaping forkfuls of sauerkraut. Mix well. Serve as a side with grilled meat.

SALAMI, ARTICHOKE, MOZZARELLA SALAD

Start to finish: 20 minutes
Serves 4

Take a can of artichokes in water, drain, rinse, and place on a serving plate. Quarter the artichokes. Season with fresh ground pepper, Herbamare, 1 tablespoon of good-quality balsamic vinegar, and 2 tablespoons of olive oil. Mix well.

Slice the desired amount of salami into 1-inch strips and mix in with the artichokes. The quantity and variety of meat depends on preference. I use about 15 slices, and I prefer beef or pork fennel salami. Garnish with a bit of lettuce or arugula and grated carrot.

Place a large ball of creamy, fresh mozzarella in the middle of the salad dish and slice as desired. Burrata can also be used. Season with fresh ground pepper. This is a good starter for a meatless pasta main or vegetable soup dish.

Variation: Cooked corkscrew pasta can also be added to the artichoke and meat to create a one-dish pasta salad meal.

CHOPPED SALAD with RED CABBAGE

Start to finish:
Serves 4–6

1½–2 cups of cooked chickpeas

Half small to medium red cabbage
1 large zucchini, cubed
Small red bell pepper, chopped
1 carrot, thinly sliced
2 scallions
½ cucumber
2 cups cooked chopped string beans
1 cup garden peas
10 cherry tomatoes, roughly chopped or halved
1 garlic clove

Salt or Herbamare
Fresh ground black pepper
Oregano
Red wine vinegar

Olive oil

Steam red cabbage. Once cooked, let it cool. Steam string beans in cabbage water for 7 minutes or so, as desired, and remove from water. Steam a cup of fresh garden peas in the same water for 3 minutes. Rinse both under cold water. Chop the string beans.

Grill:
Place cubed zucchini, chopped small red pepper, and carrot slices on a grill pan and season with a tablespoon of olive oil and lightly salt. Place under oven broiler until edges begin to brown, or as desired.

Remove and let cool.

Take a large bowl for tossing all of the vegetables. Rub the inside of the bowl with fresh garlic clove.

Chop 2 scallions and ½ a cucumber with the skin. Add them and the 1½ to 2 cups of chickpeas to the large bowl. Season liberally with with fresh ground pepper, and 2 tablespoons of red wine vinegar.

Thinly slice the red cabbage. Add to the bowl.

Add the string beans and peas.

Add 2 healthy pinches of oregano, and 10 chopped cherry tomatoes sliced in half. Add the grilled vegetables and the juice from the baking sheet, scraping all of the pan bits into the bowl too. Season with some herby salt and toss all of the vegetables together.

Eat as is or dress with a Caesar salad dressing.

GOAT CHEESE

A French staple enjoyed in London with a twist, mango chutney.

Start to finish: 20 minutes
Servings: 1 Crottin per person

Goat cheese, Crottin de Chavignol

Mango chutney or very ripe fresh mango
Tomato
Romaine
1 tablespoon vinegar

Herbamare

Olive oil

Clean the romaine. Slice the whole head on the round in 2-inch sections. Place in a large bowl. Lightly season with Herbamare and fresh ground pepper and drizzle with a bit of olive oil and vinegar. Toss.

If using mango chutney, measure out 1 cup. In a small bowl, mix the chutney with the tomatoes. Slice each crottin into three equal discs. You can scrape a bit of the wrinkly exterior off the ends to expose the cheese. When ready to serve the salad, place the cheese on a nonstick baking sheet and run the cheese under the broiler until the top slightly browns. Plate the romaine and top it with a tablespoon of the mango tomato mix and place one to three slices of grilled cheese on top of the chutney mix.

BRUSCHETTA TOPPINGS

Toppings for sliced and grilled Italian bruschetta bread or a French *grand pain*.

- Take 4 large vine-ripe tomatoes, ½ of a small brown onion, one garlic clove, 1 tablespoon of red wine vinegar, 3 tablespoons of olive oil, a bunch of fresh basil, and a quality, preferably organic, green pesto. If making your own pesto, the basic green pesto can be composed of basil, virgin olive oil, toasted pine nuts, pecorino or Parmesan cheese, lemon juice, garlic, and salt and pepper to season and mix those ingredients in a blender to a coarse pesto paste. Finely chop the basil, tomato, and onion. Add to a bowl and mix in the other ingredients; season with Vogel's Herbamare and freshly ground pepper. Let marinate overnight or at least for an hour. When serving, garnish with some fresh chopped oregano.

- White peach, prosciutto, and mozzarella cheese. Peel the peaches, core, and thinly slice. Toss with olive oil and lightly grill on both sides. Coarsely chop. Shred the prosciutto and the mozzarella. Mix with the peaches.

- Mashed broad beans mixed with ricotta and freshly chopped mint and basil leaves. Drain a can of broad beans, rinse, pat dry with a paper towel, place in a bowl, and coarsely mash with a potato masher. Mix in 1½ cups of ricotta and a handful each of chopped fresh mint and basil leaves. Add fresh ground pepper and ¼ cup of lemon juice and drizzle with olive oil. Mix well.

PENNETTE PRIMAVERA

Start to finish: 1 hour
Serves 6–8

Spinach
String beans
1 potato
Peas
Basil
1 garlic clove

Pennette
Salt
Pepper
Balsamic vinegar

Olive oil

Cut the string beans into pieces that are 1 inch or smaller. Remove any apparent strings. Place in a large skillet with the boiling water and cook for 3 minutes. Clean the spinach, chop it, and place it on top of the string beans. Add the crushed garlic clove. Peel and cube the potato (small cubes) and add to the skillet. Stir well, cover, and simmer until the potato is done, about 7 minutes. Add fresh chopped basil and season with salt, pepper, olive oil, and 1 tablespoon of balsamic vinegar.

Let simmer for 5 minutes. Add the peas and let simmer for 20 more minutes. While that is simmering, cook the pennette as desired in salt water. When done, strain and set aside. Mix cooked pennette in with the vegetables. This dish can be enhanced with a scattering of toasted pine nuts. Sprinkle with Parmesan, if using.

PACCHERI WITH ZUCCHINI SAUCE

Start to finish: 30 minutes
Paccheri is a large tube pasta.

1 large leek, cleaned and diced
2 zucchini, finely chopped
1 tablespoon fresh or dried oregano
Basil, fresh sliced
1 large garlic clove, diced
Juice of 1 lemon (*optional*)

1 cup toasted pine nuts
Chili flakes
½ cup white wine (*optional*)
1 tablespoon cornstarch or nutritional yeast (*optional*)

3 tablespoons olive oil
2 cups cream or oat milk

This is a really simple, tasty, and filling pasta dish. The oat-milk option is for those who are dairy free.

Place the olive oil in a large pan and lightly salt. Heat the oil over medium heat. Sauté all of the vegetables and herbs in the olive oil. You want the leeks to brown and the zucchini to melt into the oil. Once the vegetables are browned, optionally you can deglaze with the lemon juice or with the white wine—do not use both. Place on a very low heat, cover, and let simmer while you prepare the sauce and pasta.

Boil 12 tubes of pasta. While that is boiling, place the cream or oat milk in a blender and blend it with the pine nuts. Depending on the thickness desired, you can add a bit, a tablespoon or less, of cornstarch or nutritional yeast to the blender too. Pour the blended mixture over the vegetables. Let simmer uncovered.

Drain the pasta tubes. If not dairy free, toss the pasta with some salted butter. Place the pasta tubes in the sauce. Coat the pasta with the sauce. There should be ample sauce to cover and fill the pasta. Garnish if desired with a pinch of red chili flakes.

KINDA CALLALOO

Prep time: 1 hour 40 minutes
My amalgam of vegetable stew influences from Africa and the southern United States with inspiration from West Indian callaloo.
Serves 4

Black-eyed peas

White or green cabbage, chopped
1 red pepper, deseeded and chopped
Spinach, chopped
1 small carrot, finely chopped
Scallion, chopped
2 garlic cloves, finely chopped
1 yellow onion, chopped
Scotch bonnet pepper, whole
Thyme
Sorrel (if available)

Bay leaf
Peppercorns

Groundnut oil

Heat ½ cup of oil, and season with salt and peppercorns. Add the onion, and cook to brown slightly. Add the remaining vegetables. Give a good stir for a few minutes, letting the flavors mix. Cover with a very tight lid and simmer for 20 minutes. You want the vegetables to steam in their own juices.

After 20 minutes, add the cooked black-eyed peas; drain and rinse one 400g/8oz can. You can remove the Scotch bonnet pepper at this point if you do not want the dish to be too hot.

It can then be used to garnish the dish or discarded. Cover again with the tight lid and continue cooking on low heat for 40 minutes. Or, you can move the casserole to a 160°C/325°F oven and leave it for an hour or so.

The following methods for preparing some of the basics are inspired by the most simple approaches I have seen to bringing out delicious natural flavors.

SPINACH
Start to finish: 10 minutes
Serves 4

400g/8 cups spinach
1 liter water
Salt

Don't cook spinach. To have flavorful spinach, full of color and taste, bring the water to a boil. Add a pinch of salt and remove from the heat. Place the cleaned spinach in the hot water and steep for 5 minutes. Drain the spinach, squeeze out excess water, and use as desired.

SIMPLE ASPARAGUS
Start to finish: 20 minutes
Serves 4

20 or so green asparagus
1 large garlic clove
Juice of ½ a lemon

Balsamic vinegar

Olive oil

Rinse the asparagus.

Cut each stem into four sections, discarding the hard ends.

Thinly slice 1 large garlic clove. Mix in with the asparagus. Add the lemon juice, being careful not to let any seeds remain.

Heat 4 tablespoons of olive oil. Add the asparagus and freshly ground salt and pepper, as desired, and sauté for 5 minutes. Stir in 1 tablespoon of balsamic vinegar. Sauté for another 3 minutes. Add ½ cup water, stir, cover, and let steam for 2 minutes. Remove from the heat and leave covered.

Variation: Steamed string beans are a nice addition to this to create a green medley.

MASHED POTATOES
Start to finish: 30 minutes
Serves 4–6

4 large potatoes

Garlic clove

Bouillon cube, poultry or vegetable *(optional)*
Fresh ground black pepper or white pepper

Butter
Crème fraîche or heavy cream

Peel the potatoes. Cut into quarters for quicker cooking. If increasing the recipe, for every four potatoes, have a garlic clove.

Boil potatoes and garlic in salted water (a bouillon cube can also be added), until the potatoes are falling apart.

Strain once cooked through.

Return the potatoes and garlic to the pan. On low heat, mash with a masher. Once thoroughly mashed, you will need a wooden spoon to stir and whip the potatoes.

Add salt, fresh ground black pepper or white pepper, 75g/3 tablespoons of butter per 4 potatoes.

Continue stirring. Then stir in a heaping tablespoon of crème fraîche or ¼ cup of heavy cream, more or less until desired consistency. Whip in until desired consistency.

CAULIFLOWER MASH

Start to finish: 40 minutes
Serves 4

Florets of 1 cauliflower head
1 large garlic clove

White pepper

Grated white cheese, cheddar or Ossau-Iraty
Butter

Put garlic and a pinch of salt or a vegetable bouillon cube in a deep saucepan. Just cover with hot water and bring to a boil. As soon as the water is boiling, add the potatoes. Halfway through their cooking, add the cauliflower. Once the potatoes and cauliflower are both soft, strain—reserve a cup of the cooking water. Put the vegetables (don't forget the garlic clove) back in the saucepan, and over low heat begin to mash. Once mashed, stir until any excess water is absorbed. Add some white pepper and about ½ cup of grated cheese and butter as desired and mix well.

CARROT MASH
Start to finish: 30 minutes
650g/1.5 pounds carrots

Salt
White pepper *(optional)*

Butter *(optional)*

This mash literally tastes like sweet potato mash. Clean and peel the carrots, then roughly cut into sections. Boil in salted water. Once boiled and strained, return the carrots to the pan and mash them. They then have to remain on the heat until the excess water evaporates. Stir frequently so the carrot does not burn on the bottom. Season with white pepper and butter, as desired.

Variation: Fold 2 stiffened egg whites into mash. Apportion the mixture into nonstick muffin tins and bake in preheated 170°C/350°F oven until firm. Serve as a side vegetable, like a mini terrine.

VEGETABLE MEDLEY
(Beef Wellington side dish)

Start to finish: 30 minutes
Serves 4–6

> 4 cups sugar snap peas
> 1 cup peas
> 1 medium carrot, sliced into ¼-inch discs
> 1 large potato, chopped into 1-inch chunks

Freshly ground sea salt

Olive oil

Place carrot in boiling water.

Cook potato with carrot for 10 minutes.

Drain.

Bring more water to a boil and immerse the sugar snap peas and peas. Boil for 3 minutes.

Drain.

Put all of the vegetables back into the pan and season with sea salt and a drizzle (up to ¼ cup) of olive oil. Cover and let cook in its own heat.

RADICCHIO WITH SCALLION, GARLIC, AND POTATO

Start to finish: 30 minutes

    4 potatoes of baking size
    1 small radicchio head
    4 spring onions, chopped
    2 garlic cloves
    Olive oil

Peel, clean, and dice the potatoes. I dice the potatoes into about 10 pieces per potato, but you can cut them as you like. Sliced works equally as well. Heat about ¼ cup of olive oil in a skillet, and add the potatoes and crushed garlic cloves. Sauté; you want the potatoes to crisp on each side. Season with salt and pepper while cooking. Add the scallions about halfway through cooking the potatoes. When done, remove from the pan. Keep the pan on a low heat. Clean the radicchio, remove the hard stem center and coarsely break up the leaves. Stir-fry the radicchio in the same skillet as the potatoes, for no more that 3 to 4 minutes. You just want to heat the radicchio through and get it to slightly wilt. Add a splash of balsamic vinegar, and more olive oil if you like. Remove. Serve the potatoes on the radicchio.

CORN AND SCALLION POLENTA

I always make too much of this. Polenta goes far. I add this vegan dish to a vegetarian buffet. Great to make when corn is in season.

Start to finish: 40 minutes
Serves 8

2 cups Polenta
4 corn ears, husked
2 spring onions, finely chopped

Vegetable bouillon cube

Olive oil

Sauté the corn kernels and scallions in olive oil. Lightly salt and add fresh ground pepper.

Prepare the polenta according to the instructions but add bouillon cube to the water for cooking the polenta. Once this is dissolved, prepare the polenta. I constantly stir polenta. Once cooked, add the corn and scallions to the polenta. Stir well. Pour into a shallow serving dish. Let set, and serve.

SWEET POTATO ROAST
Start to finish: 1 hour
Serves 4–6

4 sweet potatoes, peeled and cubed
2 turnips, peeled and cubed
1 yellow onion, diced

Herbamare

Duck fat

Preheat oven to 220°C/425°F. Place all of the vegetables in a roasting dish. Season lightly with Herbamare. Add 2 tablespoons of duck fat. Mix well. Place in the oven and roast for 15 minutes. Reduce the heat to 170°C/350°F and cook for another 30 minutes or so until the sweet potato is cooked through.

TOLERABLE BRUSSELS SPROUTS

I intensely tolerate brussels sprouts because they are expected at holiday meals and my mother loves them. This one is for her.

Prep time: 20 minutes
Serves 6–8

    6 cups chopped greens, variety
    6 cups halved brussels sprouts
    3–4 cups pumpkin flesh
    1 garlic clove

                                        Peppercorns
                                        1 bay leaf

Preheat the oven to 200°C/400°F. Clean and chop the greens and the brussels sprouts. Place in a baking dish that has been rubbed with fresh garlic and salt. Add 2- to 3-inch cubes of fresh pumpkin, the peppercorns, and bay leaf. Mix well. Bake in the oven until the brussels sprouts are cooked through.

EASTER ZUCCHINI FRITTERS

Start to finish: 40 minutes
Serves 4

1 medium egg
1 egg white

2 large zucchini, deseeded and grated
1 tablespoon finely chopped fresh mint or chives
Lemon

1 heaping tablespoon self-rising flour

Vegetable oil
Sour cream
2 tablespoons finely grated Parmesan cheese

Salt the grated zucchini. Let sit for 20 minutes. This will draw out the water.

Place the grated zucchini in a sieve and rinse with cold water to remove the salt. Pat dry in batches, squeeze out excess water. Leave wrapped in paper towel for a few minutes to remove excess moisture.

Place zucchini in a bowl. Add the grated Parmesan, mint leaves, freshly ground pepper and a dash of salt, seasoned or kosher. Mix well. Stir in the flour. This will create a firm consistency.

Beat the egg and egg white until almost stiff, for about 5 minutes. I use a hand blender to get a stiff egg mixture.

Using a wooden spoon, stir the egg mixture into the zucchini.

Heat the oil. Season the oil with a couple pinches of kosher salt.

Place a heaping tablespoon of zucchini mixture into the hot oil. Allow to brown and turn over to cook on the other side.

When both sides are brown, remove the fritter and drain on a paper towel (to remove the excess oil).

Serve with lemon quarters and sour cream.

GRILLED VEGETABLES IN GRILLED RED PEPPER

I bought a basket of odd-shaped eggplant from my local farmers' market. The six were rather small, which inspired the following treatment:

Clean and cut each in half, lengthwise. Liberally salt them and let them sit for 20 minutes to allow the bitter juices to drain out.

Take a red bell pepper, cut lengthwise in half, and deseed.

Heat about 4 tablespoons of hearty rustic olive oil in a shallow frying pan. Season the oil with salt.

Rinse the salt off the eggplant.

Place the eggplant skin-side down in the oil. Fry for about ten minutes, turning the eggplant over midway—after 5 minutes. The eggplant should be nicely browned on both sides.

Remove to place in a bowl.

Now fry the zucchini and red pepper halves (skin-side down) in the same olive oil to brown.

Remove from the oil and place the zucchini and eggplant in a bowl and the red pepper in a baking dish. Coarsely chop up the eggplant and zucchini.

Coarsely dice two grilled artichokes, add to the bowl with the zucchini and eggplant, and toss with up to 2 tablespoons of freshly ground breadcrumbs. I make breadcrumbs by grating cold bread; brioche or a country loaf add flavor.

Place spoonfuls of the tossed eggplant, zucchini, and artichoke in the red pepper halves. The vegetables will overflow the red pepper.

Place two thick slices of fresh buffalo mozzarella over each stuffed pepper. Top with a garlic, basil, marinara sauce.

Bake in the oven at 190°C/375°F until the cheese bubbles and browns. Serve with buttered spaghettini.

OKRA CHIPS

Okra chips are simple to make, a wonderful snack, and an even more wonderful garnish when you want to add a bit of crunch to a soup, salad, or curry.

Start to finish: 60 minutes

24 okra fingers, thinly sliced

Herbamare

Vegetable oil *(optional)*

Clean the okra and remove and discard the hard end. Thinly slice the okra fingers. Place in a sieve. Rinse with hot water to remove some of the gelatinous juice from inside the okra. Spread on a large baking sheet. Lightly season with Herbamare and drizzle with oil if using. Bake in the oven at 170°C/350°F.

It can take up to 60 minutes for the okra pieces to become crispy. The pan will brown. Keep an eye on the okra every 20 minutes or so to push them around and turn over in the pan as necessary. When done, they will be dry and crunchy.

ZUCCHINITOUILLE WITH FRIED EGGPLANT

Start to finish: 75–90 minutes
Serves 4–6

1 eggplant
5 or 6 zucchini, cleaned and sliced in 6 sections each
2 smallish yellow onions, chopped
1 small potato, diced
1 cup parsley, chopped
Lemon

1 bay leaf
Salt
1 teaspoon garlic powder
1 teaspoon Herbes de Provence

Sunflower oil
Olive oil

Cut off the ends of the eggplant. Thinly slice and salt on each side. Let the bitter juices run off for 20 minutes.

Heat a large casserole on medium. Add all of the ingredients, except the eggplant. Mix well and cover with a tight lid. Reduce heat to low and let simmer. This can also be done in the oven at 170°C/350°F. Rinse the salt off the eggplant. Pat dry.

Coat a large skillet with sunflower oil and add about a tablespoon of olive oil. Lightly salt the oiled pan. Fry the eggplant on both sides in the skillet. You may need to top up the vegetable oil from time to time. Arrange the cooked eggplant around the edges of a serving dish. Place the zucchini stew in the center of the dish. Garnish with lemon wedges.

SWEET POTATO PANCAKES
15 minutes start to finish
Serves 4

2 orange sweet potatoes
Scallions, in julienne slices

Herbamare

Peanut or sunflower oil

A simple, great option for meatless days. Grate parboiled peeled sweet potatoes, and mix with scallions to your taste. Season with Herbamare. Form 4 pancakes with the mix, more if the potatoes were large. A pancake should be a handful of potato mix. Flatten into a pancake shape and fry on each side in shallow oil until crispy on the edges. The sugar in the potato will add a nice crispy glaze.

SPINACH AND PEANUT SAUTÉ
Start to finish: 60 minutes or so
Serves 2

½ cup chopped yellow onion
½ cup raw peanuts
1 large bunch fresh spinach, washed and chopped (4 cups)
2 tablespoons olive oil

Heat oil in a large sauté pan. Stir in the onion and cook until translucent. Meanwhile, chop the nuts in a food processor until finely chopped. Stir the nuts into the onion, stirring constantly until the onions and peanuts are well browned. Add the raw spinach and stir constantly until the spinach is wilted and coated with the onions and peanuts.

Variation: Can garnish with a little chopped red chili.

SCANDI NEW POTATOES

Prep time: 30 minutes
Serves 8

Caviar

New potatoes
Cooked beetroot

Liquid smoke

Sour cream

Peel and boil the new potatoes. Cut in half, lengthwise. Set aside. Mix sour cream with liquid smoke. Lightly salt and pepper the potatoes. Pour the smoky cream over the potatoes. Thinly slice the beet. Serve the potatoes on the beet and garnish each serving with a teaspoon of caviar.

MEATY SPROUTS WITH BACON AND TURNIPS

Start to finish: 60–70 minutes
Serves 4–6

2 cups pork lardons

400g/4 cups brussels sprouts
2 turnips

Herbamare

Carefully trim the hard end of the brussels sprouts. You don't want the leaves to fall off the sprouts on trimming the end. Steam 400g/4 cups brussels sprouts for 10 minutes. Cut in half. Place in a baking dish. Peel the turnips, cut into cubes, and mix with the sprouts. Add the lardons. Season with a bit of Herbamare, mix well, and bake on 200°C/400°F for 20 minutes, stir, then reduce oven temperature to 170°C/350°F and let cook for another 30 to 40 minutes.

POTATO MUFFINS

Start to finish: 30–40 minutes
Serves 12

12-muffin baking tin
6 cups room-temperature mashed potatoes

White pepper
Flour

1 cup shredded white cheddar cheese
Butter
Olive oil
¾ cup sour cream

Season leftover mashed potatoes with white pepper and salt to taste, the cheese and sour cream. Mix well.

Butter a muffin tin on the bottom and on all sides.

Preheat the oven to 180°C/350°F.

Take a handful of potato mix and make a ball. Dip in the flour and coat on all sides. Shake off excess flour. Place in a muffin cup of the tin and lightly flatten the top. Do this until all 12 muffin cups are full.

Brush the top of each potato muffin liberally with olive oil.

Place in the middle of the oven and bake until lightly golden on the top.

Serve with steamed cabbage, carrot, and broccoli.

Entrées

COD WITH POTATOES
Start to finish: 65 minutes
Serves 4

For a family-size serving, 600 to 500g (1 pound) of fresh cod loin.

Clean the fish, pierce the flesh in several places with a fork, and place it on aluminum foil. To minimize cleanup, marinate the fish on foil that can be thrown away when done. Season the fish with lemon juice, Herbamare, salt, and pepper and set aside to marinate.

Set the oven to 200°C/400°F. Heat a baking dish in the oven while preparing the potatoes so that it will be hot when ready to put the potatoes in the oven. This allows the potatoes to crisp nicely on the bottom too. You want a baking dish that will tightly hold the potatoes and fish.

Peel 3 baking potatoes and slice them down with a mandoline. This way, they are rather thin so they cook quickly and easily. Then season the potatoes with one large clove of fresh crushed garlic, lots of nice chopped flat leaf parsley, sea salt, pepper, and some olive oil. Remove the hot dish from the oven and arrange the potatoes in the dish. Run this in the oven for 20 to 30 minutes so that essentially the potatoes are cooked before putting the cod on top of it with lemon juice and crème fraîche.

I love pepper. It is a spice that people use thinking it is spicy or upsets your stomach, but there are so many different types of pepper you can use to influence the flavor, rather than the heat, of the dish you are making. My all-time favorite pepper is by Hediard, a French specialty food manufacturer. It is their tropical blend of pepper that is phenomenal on any food you put it on.

There will be a nice crisp action going on with the bottom of the potatoes. After their cooking time, remove from the oven.

The cod has now been marinating for about ½ an hour. As soon as I am close to dinner, I will put the cod on top of the cooked potatoes in parchment paper or aluminum foil. Place the potatoes on parchment in a rectangular baking dish. Evenly layer them along the central length of the dish. Place the cod on top of the potatoes. Use about 75g of butter to distribute on the fish; which is about 3 pats of butter. Also, add a few dollops of crème fraîche to the top of the fish before baking. Fold up the sides of the paper or foil and roll to close the edges to encase the fish. For those who are dairy free, the butter and cream can be left out. The cod will take about 20 minutes to bake back in the preheated oven.

Serve with steamed string beans.

TUNA STEAK
Start to finish: 40 minutes
Serving size: 150g per steak

Fresh tuna fillet, weight to vary

1 ripe mango
1 ripe papaya
1 red chili, chopped
Juice of 1 lemon

Apple cider vinegar

Olive oil

Clean the tuna steak. Lay the tuna on a piece of aluminum foil on a flat surface, pat dry, and pierce the flesh in several places with a fork. Season with a pinch of salt, fresh ground pepper, lemon juice, and a couple of tablespoons of olive oil.

Let sit while you make the salsa.

Dice the flesh of 1 mango and ½ a papaya. Place in a bowl to mix. Garnish with a teaspoon of chopped red chilis—choose a chili whose heat you can handle. Blend some olive oil, pinch of salt, pepper, and 2 tablespoons of apple cider vinegar to make a light vinegar. Stir into the fruit.

Chargrill the tuna under the broiler or in a ridged pan. I always prefer oven broiling as cleanup is easier. This works for swordfish as well.

Grill the tuna, on both sides, under a broiler. Timing depends on whether you want it well done or pink. I like to have a bit of crisping on the edges of the meat. Serve with the salsa.

SWORDFISH WITH SESAME SLAW

While lists can make shopping efficient, always be prepared to improvise. A salad Nicoise was transformed into a swordfish surprise when on arriving at the fishmonger I learned that the tuna had sold out that morning. Lesson learned to shop early to avoid surprises. I decided to take the next best, maybe better, catch: swordfish.

Preparation time: 90 minutes
Serves 4–6

500g slice fresh swordfish

½ large ripe papaya
Arugula
Datterini or San Marco tomatoes
Kalamata olives
Lime

Fish marinade:
Prepare a dry mix of salt, fresh ground pepper, ½ teaspoon of garlic powder, and ½ teaspoon paprika

Juice of one lemon
Coating of olive oil

Rinse off the fish and place on a small glass or metal dish with sides, just large enough to hold the fish, for marinating. Marinate the night before if possible or at least 2 hours before cooking. Pierce the flesh on both sides with a fork. Pour the rub on one side of the fish and rub into the flesh over the entire surface. Then pour the lemon juice over the fish, and about 2 tablespoons of olive oil. Turn over so that you are able to rub the other side of the fish. Cover and set aside in the refrigerator to marinate.

When ready to cook the fish, use the oven broiler with fan function. This will set the oven to a temperature of approximately 220°C/425°F. Remove the fish from the refrigerator 20 minutes prior to cooking. Line a pan for grilling with a large piece of aluminum foil; enough to wrap the sides up around the fish when done. Place the tomatoes on the foil and place in the oven while it is warming up about ten minutes before baking the fish. You do not want to completely cook the tomatoes ahead of the fish. Remove the tomatoes from the oven and place the fish in the center of the pan, score the fish in the center but not to completely cut in half; pour the marinade over the fish, and surround with the tomatoes. Broil the fish in the oven for approximately 5 minutes; place on the middle rack in the oven and not on the top, which would be too close to the broiler. After 5 minutes remove the fish from the oven and turn over to broil on the other side for 5 minutes. Also turn the tomatoes over at the same time as the fish. Remove from the oven and pull up the sides of the aluminum foil to enclose the fish as much as possible. Place in a dish or bowl to tightly seal with a sheet of aluminum foil or lid. Allow the fish to rest for 20 minutes or so or until ready to prepare.

To serve, slice the swordfish about half an inch thick, with a sharp non-serrated knife, slice the papaya and squeeze lime juice over it, then arrange on a bed of arugula with papaya slices and slaw. Mix the tomatoes with the black olives for an extra garnish. The papaya and swordfish are a wonderful combination.

Sesame Slaw to serve with Swordfish:
Whisk together:

½ cup toasted sesame oil
¼ cup peanut oil
¼ cup rice wine vinegar

Salt and pepper to taste
In a bowl, mix:
2 cups finely grated white cabbage
2 cups finely grated red cabbage
1 cup grated carrot

Pour the dressing over the slaw and mix well. A tablespoon of toasted sesame seeds can be added if desired. Let sit. Make the day before, if possible, stirring from time to time.

FISH FILLETS IN FENNEL SAUCE

Prep time: 40 minutes
Serves 8

8 fish fillets

Fennel bulb, finely sliced
Leeks, finely sliced (*optional*)
Lemon
Herbs, such as flat leaf parsley

2 cups flour
1 teaspoon garlic powder
1 teaspoon paprika
Polenta (*optional*)

Olive oil
Butter (*optional*)

Cut the small ragged tail end off the fish. I freeze and keep for making fish stock when needed. Slice the fish into palm-size portions. Rinse and place in a bowl. Season with salt, pepper, garlic powder, and paprika. Then coat each portion of fish with flour. You can mix the flour with super finely ground polenta for the coating. If going this route, I would suggest 1 tablespoon of polenta mixed with 1 cup of flour. You want the coating to adhere to all of the fish. Coat well and let set in the refrigerator while you prepare the fennel.

Heat some olive oil and a pat of butter in a large skillet. Lightly salt the oil. When hot, add the fennel and sauté for about 10 minutes. I sometimes also add leek to the fennel. Add finely diced herbs. I use flat-leaf parsley. The vegetables should start to lightly brown. When this happens, add about ¼ cup of lemon juice and a splash of white wine if desired. Season with salt and pepper to taste. Add the boiling water to make a sauce. Stir well and remove from the heat and set aside.

In another skillet, heat 1 cup of vegetable oil on a medium setting. Salt the oil. When oil is good and hot, take the fish fillets and lightly fry the fish on both sides. This will take about 3 minutes per side. Serve on top of the fennel.

TARTAR SAUCE
Serves 4

¾–1 cup mayonnaise
1 long shallot, finely diced
1 tablespoon capers or caper berries, finely diced
4 cornichons, finely diced
¼ cup finely diced curly parsley
1 teaspoon chopped fresh dill
½ teaspoon garlic powder
Fresh ground pepper
Pinch salt

Mix all of the ingredients together in a bowl. Chill. Serve with fish.

Variation: For a spicier version, add some diced jalapeño.

FRIED CHICKEN WITH SPANISH RICE

Start to finish: 90 minutes
Serves 6–8

1 chicken

2 onions, chopped
8 fresh plum tomatoes, deseeded, chopped
1 green pepper, finely chopped
2 jalapenos, deseeded and chopped
1 bay leaf
1 cup of freshly chopped coriander/cilantro
3 garlic cloves, diced
2–3 tablespoons tomato paste

1 tablespoon Ma Bell's poultry seasoning
1 teaspoon paprika
1 tablespoon flour
3 tablespoons apple cider vinegar
500 g/4 cups cooked rice
1 level tablespoon cumin powder
1 level tablespoon thyme
Tomato paste
1 chicken stock cube
Maggi liquid seasoning

Peanut oil
Olive Oil
Grated white cheese (white cheddar, Monterey Jack,
or Cantal)

Butterfly or cut the chicken into several pieces. Place in a bowl and season with salt, pepper, 1 tablespoon of Ma Bell's, the paprika, the flour, and the apple cider vinegar. Mix well to coat the chicken. Let sit for 20 minutes.

In a large skillet with a cover, heat a mixture of ½ cup of peanut oil and ¼ cup of olive oil. Fry the chicken pieces in the skillet. You want each side to brown. I also begin by cooking the chicken skin-side down. When done, remove the chicken from the skillet and place it in a baking dish to go in the oven. Set aside in a warm oven to continue cooking through for about 20 to 30 minutes.

The rice, cheese, and chicken will come together at the end.

In the same skillet on medium heat, add all of the fresh ingredients and remaining seasoning (the cumin, thyme, chicken stock cube, tomato paste, splash of Maggi). Stir well. Cook for about 30 minutes, stirring occasionally until the onions are soft. Stir in the cooked rice, ensuring all of the grains are coated. Cover with a tight lid and let that simmer for a few minutes.

There should be a slight charring of the rice on the bottom. You can always add drops of water during the cooking to prevent burning and sticking to the bottom of the pan. Once the rice and vegetables are nicely steamed, sprinkle cheese on top, at least 1 cup, and cover the pan again. Remove from the heat and let the cheese melt over the top of the rice.

Serve with the chicken and a simple Bibb lettuce salad.

CORIANDER CHICKEN

Start to finish: 2 hours
Serves 6

1 chicken

3 cups chopped fresh coriander/cilantro
1 large onion, chopped
6 small/medium baking potatoes

Chili powder
Garlic powder
2 bay leaves
Ma Bell's poultry seasoning
1 cup cilantro-spiced olives
(may also be called coriander-spiced olives)

9 tablespoons salted butter

Season 1 stick of soft butter with 1 teaspoon each of salt, pepper, chili powder, garlic powder, 2 teaspoons of Ma Bell's, and the bay leaves. Clean the chicken. Peel and quarter six potatoes.

Preheat the oven to 220°C/425°F.

In a large deep baking dish, toss the onions, potatoes, and chopped cilantro. Season with salt and pepper.

Place the chicken, butterflied or quartered, on top of the potatoes and onions. Rub the chicken down with the seasoned butter. Be sure to get under the skin. Let sit for 20 minutes. Pour 1 cup of water into the dish. Bake for 20 minutes. Reduce the oven temperature to 200°C/400°F, add one cup of cilantro pitted olives, and continue baking for 1 hour.

Remove from the oven and carefully stir the chicken and potatoes to mix the flavors. Cover and let sit for 20 more minutes before serving. Serve with couscous or sourdough bread.

QUICK CHICKEN TAJINE

Start to finish: 90 minutes to 2 hours
Serves 4–6

2 small chickens, quartered

4 small/medium onions finely chopped
1 bunch of coriander/cilantro, chopped
12 prunes
2 garlic cloves

Maggi liquid seasoning
2 bay leaves
Cinnamon stick
Cumin powder
1 tablespoon honey
Saffron

Place the chicken pieces in a heavy casserole with a tight lid. Season with salt, pepper, 1 tablespoon of cumin powder, 3 slivers of cinnamon bark, bay leaf, and onions. I crush the bay leaf loosely in my hand. Add a little more salt, the garlic, eight threads of saffron, and 2 cups of coarsely chopped cilantro. Let sit for 20 minutes.

Place the casserole with the chicken on a medium-high heat for 10 minutes or less, stirring occasionally. The juice from the onions should form a good liquid base. Place a tight lid on to cover, lower the heat and let simmer for an hour. Remove the chicken pieces and run under the broiler to brown the skin.

While the chicken is broiling, bring the sauce to a low boil so excess water will start to evaporate. Crush the now soft cloves in the sauce. Cook uncovered while the chicken is broiling,.

When the chicken is brown, put it back in the casserole along with the pan juices. Add the prunes and honey and mix the contents of the casserole well. Let the sauce reduce.

Garnish with toasted sesame seeds or toasted almond slices if desired. Serve with warm bread and couscous.

JALAPEÑO CHICKEN BREASTS

Start to finish: 90–100 minutes
Serves 6

6 chicken breasts

½ cup chopped black kalamata olives
½ cup chopped coriander/cilantro
½ cup curly parsley
2 crushed garlic cloves
1 can chopped tomatoes
1 medium chopped onion
1 cup jalapenos, chopped

1 tablespoon cumin powder

1 cup white cheddar grated
1 cup sour cream
Peanut oil

Sauté the parsley and cilantro in 2 tablespoons of oil. Season with a bit of salt, pepper, and cumin powder. Add the garlic. Cook covered on low for about 20 minutes. Then stir in the olives and continue to cook for about 10 minutes. Place in a bowl and let cool down. Retain the skillet to cook the sauce.

Preheat the oven to 180°C/350°F.

Brown the onions on a medium heat in the same pan as the herbs. Add about another tablespoon of oil. Season with a bit of salt and pepper and 1 teaspoon of cumin powder. When brown, add the tomatoes and jalapeños and then the sour cream. Let simmer, with a loose lid, for at least 15 minutes. Remove from the heat.

Clean breasts and cut open along the length to make a pocket for the herbs. Spread the cooled-down parsley/garlic/cilantro herbs in the flesh. Place the breasts, skin-side up, in a baking dish. Season lightly with salt and pepper.

Pour the tomato sauce over the breasts. Sprinkle the grated cheddar evenly over the chicken and sauce. Bake for 45 minutes.

Serve with fried potatoes or steamed white rice.

EVERYDAY STUFFED CHICKEN
Start to finish: 2 hours
Serves: 6–8

1 chicken

½ green pepper, diced
½ cup curly parsley, chopped
1 celery stalk, finely chopped
1 medium onion, chopped
2–3 cups of whole chestnuts
2 carrots, peeled
2 large baking potatoes, peeled

1 piece of dry toast broken into crouton size pieces,
or 1 cup plain croutons
Ma Bell's poultry seasoning
1 teaspoon thyme
1 teaspoon rosemary
1 bay leaf
6 peppercorns

4 tablespoons salted butter

Sauté the herbs, seasoning, and vegetables in the butter. Leave to simmer for 20 minutes. Add the chestnuts and let the mixture cool down.

Stuff one roaster chicken with the completely cooled-down chestnut stuffing. Mix about 2 tablespoons of the chestnut stuffing with the croutons. Add a bit of water to moisten the bread. You want to get all of the buttery residues up in the bread. Stuff this little bread stuffing in the neck area of the bird and fold the skin over it to hold it in place.

In the roasting pan, add two carrots and two peeled and halved baking potatoes. Lightly season the potatoes with Herbamare. Dust the skin of the stuffed chicken with Ma Bell's, salt, and pepper. Add the water to the pan. Roast for 90 minutes at 200°C/400°F. Baste chicken and potatoes twice during the baking at intervals. Reduce oven temperature to 180°C/350°F and bake for another ½ hour.

Serve with peas, Dijon mustard, and a baguette.

GIRLS' NIGHT CHICKEN
Start to finish: 3½ hours
Serves 6–8

1 large farm-raised bird with giblets

Juice of half a large juicy lemon
Fresh thyme
3 medium garlic cloves, sliced
½ leek, white part only, thinly sliced on the round
(in discs)

2 tablespoons poultry seasoning

½ stick butter

Preheat the oven to 230°C/450°F.

Let the bird rest outside the fridge until it comes to room temperature. Remove giblets and clean.

Rub the bird with the poultry seasoning, salt, thyme, and pepper.

Liberally place slices of garlic cloves under the skin and inside the bird. I also slightly season the cavity of the bird with a little salt and pepper. Place the liver in the cavity of the bird, along with any other giblets you like. I keep the neck to make chicken stock for soup.

Pour the juice of the lemon over the bird. Distribute the slices of leek over the bird. Lightly salt the leeks.

Place pats of butter on the breasts, legs. Add a teaspoon more thyme.

Place the bird in the preheated oven. Reduce the temperature to 165°C/325°F once the oven is closed.

Let the bird slow roast for approximately 3 hours.

Serve with butter lettuce leaves tossed with olive oil and balsamic vinegar.

CHICKEN SKEWERS

Start to finish: 2½ hours
Serves 4

6–8 chicken thigh fillets
Thick plain yogurt

6 garlic cloves, crushed
Juice of one lemon
4 small red bell peppers
4 plum tomatoes
1 large carrot, ribboned
¼ red cabbage, shredded
Leaves of 2 Bibb lettuce

1 chicken bouillon cube
2 teaspoons sumac
Hummus

Olive oil

Rinse thighs and cut lengthwise and then across, dividing each thigh into four or six pieces, according to the preferred size of meat to skewer.

Combine lemon juice, crushed garlic, and bouillon cube and mix well. Stir in one heaping tablespoon of thick natural yogurt (I like Skyr and Fage/Total). Then mix with the chicken pieces in a flat dish. Season with salt, freshly ground black pepper, and sumac. Marinate 20–30 minutes, and of course this can be done for longer.

Set the oven to 185°C/375°F.

Soak several wooden skewers in cold water. These will be used later for the chicken. Soaking ensures that the flesh does not adhere to the wood.

Clean, halve, and deseed 4 red peppers. Place on a baking tray and drizzle with olive oil, then salt and pepper.

Let these brown in the oven for 20 minutes, skin-side up. Then lower oven temperature to 170°C/350°F. Turn the peppers so they are skin-side down and return to oven.

When ready to cook the chicken skewers, remove the baking tray with the peppers from the oven. Place the chicken skewers on the now soft and lightly browned red peppers.

Return to the oven and cook for 30 minutes, turning the skewers over 20 minutes in. After 30 minutes turn the oven off and place fresh tomato halves in baking dish alongside the chicken and leave in the oven for another 15 minutes.

Lightly toss a salad of carrot ribbons, shredded red cabbage, and a green leaf with a tablespoon of apple cider vinegar. Serve the peppers and chicken skewers on the salad with a garnish of hummus and the roasted tomatoes.

Serve with warm pita bread.

EASY ENCHILADAS

Start to finish: 2½ hours
Makes 6 enchiladas

4 boneless chicken thighs

1 celery stalk, finely chopped
¾ cup diced red pepper
1 diced small onion
1 tablespoon chopped parsley
1–2 tablespoons chopped coriander/cilantro
1 can chopped tomatoes
1 cup chopped black olives to garnish

1 heaping tablespoon cumin powder
1 teaspoon chili powder
1 teaspoon garlic powder
1 level tablespoon thyme
½ chicken bouillon cube
corn tortillas
1 cup long grain rice
2 cups cooked black beans

Peanut oil
Sour cream or natural Greek yogurt
Grated white cheese of choice, Cantal or cheddar

Preheat oven to 220°C/425°F. Place the chicken thighs in a shallow dish, for oven and stovetop, with a cover. Mix the cumin, chili, garlic powder, and thyme. Lightly dust each thigh with the seasoning mix. Place the chopped vegetables and herbs over the chicken. Lightly season the vegetables with the seasoning mix. Add the chopped tomatoes and again lightly dust with the seasoning mix. Crush the bouillon cube and sprinkle over the tomatoes. Drizzle about 2 tablespoons of peanut oil over the tomatoes. Cover the dish with aluminum foil, tightly sealing the foil around the pan edges, and cover with a heavy lid.

Bake for 20 minutes. Remove from the oven, uncover, and stir the contents of the dish. Re-cover tightly. Turn the oven temperature down to 160°C/325°F and let slow cook for up to 90 minutes or more. The heavy lid will seal in the moisture. You can check on the dish and stir halfway through the baking, if desired. When done, the chicken will shred very easily.

Shred the chicken and set aside in a bowl, leaving the sauce in the pan.

Place a corn tortilla in a baking dish. Fill with 1 tablespoon of black beans, some chicken, and shredded cheese. Roll to close and repeat. Spoon the sauce from the pan over the enchiladas and coat as desired with shredded cheese. I only add about ¾ cup of cheese. Bake in the oven 15 to 20 minutes.

While that is baking, add the long-grain rice to the pan in which you baked the chicken with any remaining sauce. Toss in any extra black beans. Add the boiling water, stir well, and cook the rice on low heat. The rice will take approximately 20 minutes to cook. After 15 minutes, add a bit of hot water if needed.

Serve each enchilada over the rice. Garnish as desired with black olives and sour cream or yogurt.

CHICKEN SALAD SOUP

When summertime proves too hot to turn the oven on, but you still have a taste for a Sunday roast dinner, make this easy chicken salad and cold soup from the chicken's baking broth.

Start to finish: 75 minutes
Serves 2/3

2 whole chicken legs
2 eggs

1 small shallot, diced
1 tablespoon finely diced green bell pepper
4 zucchini, coarsely chopped
1 cup fresh peas
1 leek, coarsely chopped
1 small baking potato
Fresh mint

Celery salt
Herbes de Provençe
Mustard
Mayonnaise

Olive oil
Crème fraîche

Preheat oven to 170°C/350°F. Place the two chicken legs (thigh and drumstick) in aluminum foil and season with salt, pepper, celery salt, and Herbes de Provence. Loosely enclose the chicken in the foil and bake for 45 minutes.

While the chicken is baking, boil 2 eggs. Once the eggs are ready, peel, chop and add them to a mixing bowl with the shallot and green pepper.

Soup:
In a stockpot, place the zucchini, peas, leek, potato, and bouillon cube. Dry sauté for 5 minutes or less and add 2 cups of
water. Simmer for 20 minutes, until the potato begins to break
down and the liquid level is just above the vegetables. Remove
from the heat. Blend the soup with a hand blender. Add 1
tablespoon of crème fraîche. Let cool. When ready to serve,
rub the bottom of each soup bowl with a mint leaf, ladle in the
soup serving, and garnish with finely chopped mint.

Once the chicken is baked, remove from the oven and let it
sit for 10 minutes. Then open the foil and the chicken will be
sitting in at least 1 good cup of its juice/broth. Remove the
meat from the bones and skin and set aside on a plate, leaving
the skin and bones in the broth in the foil. Chop the meat as
coarsely or as finely as you like, let cool for 10 minutes or so,
and mix with the hard-boiled egg, shallot, and green pepper.
Set aside.

Return to the soup with the chicken broth in the foil and pour
the liquid into the soup, not letting the skin or bones go into
the soup. Stir well. You can now discard the bones, skin, and
foil.

Season the chicken, green pepper, shallot, and hard-boiled
eggs with 1 tablespoon of apple cider vinegar, freshly ground
pepper, 1 teaspoon of Dijon mustard, and mayonnaise (I
would use about 3 tablespoons) as desired. Let chill in the
refrigerator.

Variation: A few chopped cornichon can also be added to the
chicken salad. To vary the flavor of the chicken, the legs can
also be seasoned with some chopped tarragon leaves, or curry
powder, or anything you fancy in your chicken salad.

SMOKED CHICKEN FRIED RICE

Start to finish: 45 minutes
Serves 2

1 smoked chicken breast
1 medium egg

1 yellow onion, diced
1 tablespoon grated fresh ginger (*optional*)
2 garlic cloves, crushed
1 red chili, split lengthwise and deseeded
½ cup diced spring onions
1 cup diced green bell pepper
1 cup fresh garden peas
1 cup diced carrots
½ cup diced string beans

Light soy sauce
Fish sauce
Rice wine vinegar
2 cups cold, cooked Thai jasmine rice

Sesame oil
Groundnut oil

Finely slice the smoked chicken into 2- to 3-inch julienne-style strips. It can be with or without skin, but I prefer with. Chop the red chili and mix it with the chicken. Place in the fridge while you prepare the other vegetables.

Place the wok on a low heat and add 2 tablespoons of peanut oil and 1 tablespoon of sesame oil. Salt the oil with a pinch of salt. Add the onion, garlic, ginger if using, and scallions to the wok. Stir well. I like using a perforated metal skimmer and strainer spoon; a wooden spoon also works well. A light sizzle is what you want. Remove the chicken from the fridge.

Increase the heat of the wok and let the onion brown, not caramelize. Add a couple of good dashes of rice wine vinegar once the onion begins to brown. This should create a good sizzle. Let evaporate for about 1 minute, and then add the remainder of the vegetables to the wok.

Work the spoon to mix the vegetables and onion well. Add a dash or two of fish sauce. Stir. Add the cold rice. Keep working the vegetables with the spoon so that the rice separates. Add the chicken and a tablespoon of soy sauce.

Cover the wok and lower the heat to the lowest setting. Let steam for 3 minutes or so; give the wok a slight shake halfway through. Remove the wok cover and stir in a tablespoon more of soy sauce if desired. Cover and turn heat to low.

Beat the egg in a small bowl. Remove cover from wok. Make a well at the bottom of the wok by pushing the rice to the sides. Add a few drops of oil to the bottom of the wok. Pour the egg into the well. Let bubble for not more than a minute and begin to stir the rice contents into the egg. Increase the heat to medium and continue stir-frying for about 2 minutes so that all of the flavors are nicely mingled.

Serve with garlicky bok choy or a radish salad.

ROAST DUCK

Start to finish: 115 minutes
Serves 4

4½-pound duck

1 yellow onion cut into thinly sliced discs
1 large carrot in 1-inch discs
1 tablespoon fresh thyme
1 tablespoon fresh rosemary
4–6 turnips, peeled
2 bay leaves
1 cup white wine

Preheat the oven to 220°C/425°F.

Clean the duck and place in a baking pan. Season with salt
and fresh ground pepper to taste and then toss with all of the
ingredients, leaving the white wine to pour over the vegetables
in the pan last.

Place in the oven and roast for 20 minutes on 220°C/425°F.
Reduce the oven temperature to 190°C/375°F. Then roast 75
minutes. Baste occasionally. Remove from the oven and let
rest for 15 minutes prior to serving.

DUCK
Start to finish: 2 hours

Clean duck, back split and butterflied

1 cup peas
2 spring onions, sliced
1 teaspoon grated ginger

1 teaspoon garlic powder
1 tablespoon Chinese 5-spice
2 cups smoky Chinese tea

Wash and clean giblets.

Burn pinfeathers off the bird. Score both sides with a sharp knife in several places.

To season the duck, rub the bird down with salt, garlic powder, and Chinese 5-spice powder. Place in a roasting pan.

Roast in a superhot oven for 20 minutes. Then reduce the temperature to 170°C/350°F and leave the duck to slow cook for 2 hours. During this time, baste the duck every 30 minutes with smoky Chinese tea. Excess oil can be suctioned or spooned out of the roasting pan. One hour, 20 minutes into cooking add sliced scallions, ginger, and peas that have been sautéed in the sesame oil to the roasting pan. Serve with steamed rice or noodles (soba or buckwheat).

You know the saying, "You are what you eat?" Well, the same goes for livestock. They are what they eat. The taste of their flesh is directly affected by whether they are grain-fed, grass-fed, or rubbish-fed. If fed naturally, to me, saying that meat (beef and lamb in particular) is not a plant-based food can be an oxymoron. For meat dishes, I calculate 200g/¼ pound, or less, per serving.

Ask, how were you fed?
Is your flesh pure to nature?
One is what one eats.

A London Lamb Story

I removed the boneless shoulder of lamb from the bottom shelf of my refrigerator. This is the best place to keep meat fresh, where it achieves an almost, but not quite, frozen state. I placed the shoulder next to the sink, eyeing my collection of spices with a side glance: salt, a selection of red, white, and black tropical peppercorns, bay leaf, freshly peeled garlic cloves, ground cumin, chili powder, cinnamon sticks, dried thyme, and threads of Moroccan saffron.

I turned, kneeled down, and opened the drawer to take out my glass, not wood, workboard. Unlike wood, glass does not hold memories of what came before, failures or successes; the residues from whatever was previously prepared on it wash away; it is pure and respects the flavor integrity of whatever is placed upon it. I placed it next to the sink and began to unwrap the lamb shoulder from the plastic vacuum pack. The meat nicely filled both palms of my hands so I knew it would be enough to satisfy all. I then ran cold water over it to rinse away the blood.

The lamb's shoulder back on the glass work surface, I considered what it should be cooked in. What would best hold the heat to achieve the right sauce consistency without burning the onions, while allowing the meat to cook long enough to become melt-in-your-mouth tender?

Mood, or perhaps the crisp air and fog outside, dictated that the shoulder, when done, should fall off the bone with a pull of leavened bread that could also soak up the juices.

I decided on my old enamel-coated cast-iron casserole that could be put in the oven at a high enough temperature that would allow the skin to crisp up before being transferred to finish slow cooking on the burner.

With that decided and very pleased with my choice, I set about cutting my meat down, seasoning it, placing it in the casserole and then in my oven. With the lamb where it belonged, I proceeded to pull together my spices, herbs, and onions for the sauce.

To calm my wavering over my next step, I consulted my Moroccan culinary tome that a great cook from a grand house in Morocco shared with me many years ago. I leafed to the relevant page. "*Tajine aux pruneaux—see poulet aux pruneaux.*"

The list of ingredients called for cinnamon powder. I had sticks at the ready. Now I would have to pull out the powder. Then the recipe continued and read that one adds sticks to the spice mix, not powder. But of course, it was as I had originally thought. How would someone learning to cook figure out which to use, powder or stick, if the recipe inconsistently called for ingredients? Intuition? I put the powder and sticks away. Focus renewed; these would not be for today's sauce.

Midway through marrying my chosen spices and herbs, the strong grilled smell that the cumin brought to my mix jolted me back to . . . the oven timer rang.

The crisping of the meat was over. Pulling the casserole out of the oven, I slowly surveyed the condition of the meat and whether the skin was sufficiently crackling and the onions nicely browned. Yes, ready for the burner. I mixed the remaining herbs and vegetables in with the lamb in the casserole now on the stove. I then turned to fry some sliced and deseeded tomato wedges in palm oil. The palm oil brings flavor distinctive to West African cuisine with its faint aroma and aftertaste of miniature sweet bananas. I added a generous splash of Maggi to the frying tomatoes. After 5 minutes of watching my pot, I mixed the now velvety tomato base in with my lamb stew and let it simmer.

EASY LAMB STEW
About 2½ hours slow cooking
Serves 8

1 boneless leg of lamb
2 celery stalks, finely chopped
Carrots, scrubbed and quartered
1 brown onion, finely chopped
2 garlic cloves, coarsely chopped
Fresh rosemary

¼ cup, more or less, red wine from southwest France
2 level tablespoons flour
Mustard
1 bay leaf
8 peppercorns

Wash the leg. Cut into very large chunks. Take at least 2 full stems of rosemary, coarsely chop the leaves to have 2 tablespoons, and place in a bowl with the lamb. Then season the meat with 1 heaping tablespoon of Dijon mustard, freshly ground salt as desired, and chopped garlic cloves. Mix it in with the lamb. On medium heat, dry sauté the onion for 2 minutes in a casserole that will comfortably hold the meat and has a tight lid. Add the well-seasoned meat and celery and sauté for 20 minutes—so that the fat starts to render and brown.

Do not discard the bowl the meat was in!

Add the bay leaf and peppercorns to the lamb. Continue cooking for 5 minutes or so, and then add the red wine. Raise the temperature a bit to get a small bubbling, then cover the pot with the lid and reduce the heat to simmer. Let simmer for 90 minutes, and then add the carrots and more salt if desired.

Now, place the flour in the bowl with the seasoning residue from the lamb. Whisk the cold water into the flour in the bowl and tilt the bowl around to pick up the seasonings from the sides of the bowl. Stir the floury water into the lamb to thicken the sauce. Let simmer for another 30 to 45 minutes. The sauce should be relatively thick. Serve with crusty country bread and the red wine.

The meat can be seasoned the night before to marinate. Also, the simmering can be done in the oven, rather than stovetop, at 170°C/350°F.

The following rice dish can easily become a favorite, and it is what it says—so eat sparingly if you are calorie conscious.

There are several variations with different meats but I find it best with lamb or beef.

FAST AND EASY SAVORY "FAT" RICE

Start to finish: 90 minutes
Serves 6–8

Boneless lamb shoulder
10 string beans, diced confetti size
1 small, or ½ a large carrot, diced confetti size
3 tablespoons chopped curly parsley
2 tomatoes deseeded, finely chopped
10 pitted green olives (herb and garlic flavor preferred)

1 bouillon cube
Herbes de Provence
1 tablespoon cumin powder
1 teaspoon chili powder
2 cups of onion gravy
2 cups uncooked Thai jasmine rice

Preheat oven to 250°C/475°F.

Clean the meat and lay it out flat, skin-side down. Prick the
flesh in several places with a fork and rub in salt, fresh ground
pepper, and 1 teaspoon of Herbes de Provence. Turn meat
over. Prick the fat and skin across the surface with a fork and
season with salt, pepper, Herbes de Provence, ground cumin,
and the chili powder. Massage the seasoning into the fat. Let
the meat sit for 10 minutes. Put lamb in the oven and reduce
heat to 220°C/425°F. Roast for 20 minutes. Then reduce oven
temperature to 150°C/300°F and set the timer for 1 hour.

Baste the meat with the onion gravy at 20-minute intervals.

Dry sauté the string beans, carrot, parsley, and tomatoes in a
pan with a lid, large enough to hold the cooked rice. Dry sauté
the vegetables for ten minutes and then add the rice. Mix well.

Add the boiling water, stir in the bouillon cube, reduce heat, and simmer. The rice will absorb all of the water and should cook in 20 minutes. The rice should not be wet when done. Leave covered and turn off the heat to prevent the rice burning on the bottom of the pan. Add the olives to the rice. You can give the rice a stir before leaving covered.

Check the lamb; it should be fork tender. Remove from the oven. If the rice is dry, as it should be, take some of the juice of the lamb and add to the rice to finish steaming the rice with the meat flavor. Return the rice to a low heat. The rice should finish cooking within 10 minutes. Slice the lamb down and serve over the rice.

LAMB GREEN TAJINE
Start to finish: 3 hours
Serves 6–8

1 boneless lamb shoulder

1 large onion finely chopped
12 okra, finely chopped
1 bunch (a fistful) of curly parsley
2–3 cups, chopped, fresh spinach
3 green chilis, deseeded and finely chopped
1 large garlic clove

6 threads of saffron
Medley of peppercorns (white, black)
2 tablespoons of fish sauce
1 teaspoon or fresh sprig thyme
2 small bay leaves

Okra is gelatinous, or slimy. Once it is chopped, I place in a colander and vigorously rinse with hot water to remove some of the gelatinous matter.

Dry sauté the onion, parsley, okra, and chilis on a low medium. Crush the bay leaves and sprinkle in with veggies. Salt and add 6 to 8 peppercorns, the thyme, and saffron. Sauté until the juices start to render and brown, about 10 minutes.

Clean and cut meat into chunks. Add the meat and garlic clove to the pan. Add a little more salt and sauté with the veggies for a few minutes. Let the fat of the meat brown a bit. Once meat starts to brown, add the spinach in batches and stir in until the spinach is wilted. Add the fish sauce. Cover and bring to a vigorous bubble. Then reduce heat to low and let simmer for 2 hours, stirring occasionally. Remove the lid and let the stew cook uncovered for up to 45 minutes allowing the water to evaporate and for a thicker sauce to form. Serve with white rice.

Variation: This can also be cooked in the oven at 160°C/325°F for 2 hours instead of on the stove

PRUNE TAJINE

1 kilogram/2 pounds boneless lamb shoulder

1 handful chopped parsley
1 handful chopped coriander/cilantro
12 prunes
2 small to medium onions

Saffron threads
⅓ cinnamon stick
2 tablespoons runny honey
2 tablespoons toasted sesame seeds
1 cup water

Rinse the meat off with cold water. Place on the cutting board and cut into large chunks, about twelve pieces. Using a cheese grater (you may wish to wear goggles), grate the onions onto the meat and mix the lamb and onion together. Place the meat, onions, cilantro, parsley, and cinnamon stick in a casserole where you will cook the tagine. The dish must have a tight lid. Season the meat with the desired salt, the pepper, and a generous pinch of saffron threads. Stir into the meat with a metal spoon. Place the casserole on the burner and turn the heat on to a high setting. Monitor the cooking and stir from time to time for 20 minutes. Add the water and place the tight lid on the casserole. After 3 minutes, lower the heat to a simmer and let cook for 60 minutes.

Add the prunes and honey to the stew and let simmer with the meat for 30 minutes. With a perforated spoon, remove the meat and prunes and place on a serving dish. Place the dish in a warm oven.

Let the juices in the casserole cook down until you have a saucy reduction to pour over the meat when ready to serve. Sprinkle toasted sesame seeds on the meat and prunes. This can be eaten with couscous or crusty country bread, and also goes nicely with a carrot potato mash.

MEDITERRANEAN LAMB CUTLETS
Prep time: 20 minutes
Serves 6

A rack and a half of lamb

Zest of ½ lemon
1 medium red onion, thinly sliced

1 tablespoon sumac
1 teaspoon garlic powder
1 teaspoon cumin powder
1 teaspoon fresh thyme

Clean the rack and slice into individual cutlets. Pierce the fat and flesh liberally with a sharp knife.

Place in a glass or metal bowl and add the seasonings and sliced onion. Mix the spices, onions, and meat well. Let marinate for an hour (or more, even overnight).

Preheat the oven broiler. When ready to cook, place the lamb and onion in a single layer on a baking pan. Broil for approximately 5 to 7 minutes and then turn the meat over to cook on the other side for approximately 5 minutes. The fat should be crispy. Cooking time may vary depending on taste.

Touch: For this recipe, I use hummus on the table as a garnish in place of mustard.

SUMAC LAMB

Prep time: 1 hour
Serves 8

Lamb shoulder or leg, boned

2 red onions, thinly sliced
2 cups chopped cilantro
1 tablespoon lemon rind

Sumac

Olive Oil (*optional*)

Place the onions and cilantro into a mixing bowl. Season them with salt, pepper, lemon zest, and 2 tablespoons or more of sumac. Mix well. Clean and pierce the meat in several places. The piercing is to allow the flavors to penetrate the meat. Rub the meat all over with the cilantro onion seasoning. Let marinate overnight or for a few hours if possible. If the meat is lean, drizzle a bit of olive oil. Bake in a preheated 220°C/425°F oven for 20 minutes. Reduce the temperature to 160°C/325°F and let finish roasting to desired wellness.

SPICY PENNETTE
40 minutes start to finish
Serves 6

10 fresh merguez sausages

1 large onion, chopped
1 bunch fresh basil, finely chopped
2 cups chopped parsley

1 jar Italian passata (4–5 cups)
¾ cup tomato paste
½ teaspoon granulated sugar, (*optional*)

500 g/ 1.1 lb pennette/ penne piccolo rigate (cook for 15 minutes, which is longer than directed)

Because the sausage is spicy, salty, and oily, I don't add salt, pepper, or olive oil to the sauce.

Boil the pasta in water seasoned with salt and olive oil. When done, drain and set aside.

Remove the meat from the casings. Heat a saucepan on medium heat and place the sausage in the pan, stirring with a wooden spoon to break the sausage up. Toss in the diced onion, basil, and parsley and stir. Let simmer for ten minutes and then add the passata, sugar (if using), and tomato paste. Simmer a further 20 minutes and then fold in the cooked pennette. Place in a casserole and serve.

Grated cheese is optional, but I would opt for a pecorino if using.

LAMB SHANK AND LENTILS

This reminds me of my kids' love of lamb and lentil stew, and smells that warm homes and hearts as well as cold stomachs. This easy comfort food can be prepared on the stovetop or in the oven.

Start to finish: 2–3 hours slow cooking
Serves 4

Lamb shank or two

1 large sweet onion, coarsely chopped
1 cup curly parsley, finely chopped
3 carrots, in medium slices
1 stalk organic celery, finely chopped
1 large bay leaf
1 kilogram fresh chopped tomatoes, or Pomi
2 garlic cloves
Fresh thyme

2 cups cooked lentils
1 tablespoon mustard
1 tablespoon flour

1 cup robust red wine to your taste (*optional*)
1 tablespoon olive oil (*optional*)

Get all of the vegetables sizzling in a bit of olive oil in a large stockpot on medium heat. Season with fresh ground salt and pepper. After 10 minutes, nestle the lamb shanks among the vegetables and brown the sides. Add the wine if using. Bring to a slight bubble, reduce the heat, cover, and let simmer for an hour.

Mix the flour with the water and the mustard. Add it to the pot and stir in. Continue simmering for 20 minutes. Then add the lentils. Continue cooking until the meat begins to separate from the bone. This will depend on the size of the shanks.

LAYERED LAMB

This is a lighter, but still rich, take on shepherd's pie and moussaka, the dish I so enjoyed in Greece alongside fish stew. After early-morning outings for long visits among ancient ruins, meals at seaside restaurants were a reward. The ingredients were all imbued with the energy from the Greek sun and mists of the jewel-like seas. The creamy layers of moussaka's ground lamb, potato, and sauce were a wonderful reward for tired feet.

Prep time: About 80 minutes
Serves 4–6

500g of minced lamb

1 small eggplant
1 zucchini
1 medium red onion, finely chopped
1 garlic clove
Cherry tomatoes
1 large starchy potato
1 cup fresh garden peas

1 generous teaspoon of cumin
1 tablespoon crushed mint leaves
1 tablespoon crushed dried parsley
1 tablespoon harissa
1 bay leaf

Olive oil

Preheat oven to 200°C/400°F.

Thinly slice the eggplant on the round. Salt and set aside for 20 minutes to allow the salt to draw out the bitter juices.

In a large stock pot, sauté the red onion in olive oil for 5 minutes. Add the garlic clove, ground lamb, and spices, salt to taste. Mix well so that the lamb is crumbly. Also add pepper to taste if desired. Go easy on the pepper since the harissa will add significant spice. Let this simmer for 20 minutes. Ten minutes in, add the peas, and then remove from the heat.

Thinly slice the zucchini lengthwise. Thinly slice the potato and boil in salted water for 10 minutes. Rinse the salt from the eggplant. In a large skillet, heat some olive oil, salt the oil, layer the eggplant, and fry on each side. You want the flesh to slightly char. On removing each slice of eggplant from the pan, slightly press with a spoon to drain the excess oil off the eggplant. Now slightly char the zucchini on both sides in the same pan. Remove and set aside with the zucchini and potato slices.

Layer the vegetables in a 9-inch round deep baking dish. Place the eggplant slices on the bottom, then the zucchini, then potato. In another baking dish, place the cherry tomatoes. Lightly season the tomatoes with olive oil and Herbamare. Place the tomatoes, and vegetables in the oven for about 20 minutes. You want the tomato skin to brown, so place on the top oven rack.

Remove the vegetables from the oven. Reduce the oven temperature to 170°C/350°F. Layer the lamb mince on top of the potatoes. Then layer the tomatoes on top of the lamb. They should just about cover the top of the lamb if you crush and evenly spread them over the top of the lamb.

Bake for 20 minutes. You want the juices from the lamb to run through all of the vegetables, right to the bottom. Once out of the oven, let cool for a few minutes before serving in a soup plate. This is quite filling on its own, but if a side or starter is desired, I would suggest a grated carrot or arugula salad.

Tip: The lamb or vegetables can be prepared in advance.

BEEF WELLINGTON

Start to finish: 2 hours
Serves 6–8

2 pounds beef tenderloin

2 cups diced mushroom caps
2 long shallots, diced
1 cup parsley, chopped

Garlic powder
Dijon mustard
Puff pastry
Cognac

Butter
1 cup crème fraîche

Pierce the beef all over with a fork and rub down with salt, pepper, a teaspoon of garlic powder, and 1 tablespoon of Dijon mustard. Let rest.

Roll out puff pastry to a large rectangular shape that will allow you to completely wrap the fillet.

Sauté 2 cups of sliced and diced mushroom caps in a non-stick pan on medium heat. Let the water evaporate. Add 4 tablespoons of butter along with the parsley and shallots to the mushrooms and continue cooking. Season with salt and pepper. Cover and simmer for 20 minutes. Increase heat and pour in ¾ cup of cognac. This should bubble up and reduce. Lower heat and stir in 1 cup of thick crème fraîche. Remove from heat and let cool.

In a nonstick skillet, sear the fillet on each side (about 3 minutes per side). Set aside and let cool. Heat oven to 220°C/425°F.

Roll out the pastry dough. Place the fillet in the center of the pastry. Spread the mushroom cream along the top and sides of the fillet. Fold the dough over to close in the meat. Bake at high temperature for 15 minutes and then at 190°C/375°F for the remainder of the time. I would recommend another 40 minutes because I like the beef on the well-done side. Serve with sautéed vegetables.

VEGETABLE SAUTÉ
Start to finish: 20 minutes

200g/7 ounces fresh spinach leaves
80g/3 ounces snow peas
Fresh asparagus

Herbamare
Sea salt

Olive oil

Sauté fresh spinach until water evaporates. Season with Herbamare.

To prepare the snow peas, remove the string in the side seam. Add a heaping cup of snow peas and a bunch of fresh asparagus to the spinach. Stir with 2 tablespoons of olive oil and fresh ground sea salt. Cover and let simmer/steam for 3 minutes.

This is nice with roast beef too.

Even with a wealth of knowledge of different cuisines, adding variety to weekly meals can still be challenging.

The following veal dish is easy and perfect for a Friday-night change from the usual.

FRIDAY-NIGHT VEAL

Start to finish: 90 minutes
Serves 4–6

800g/2 pounds veal fillet (tenderloin)
5 strips bacon (turkey or pork) or
thinly sliced smoked duck breast

1 small cauliflower
20 baby new potatoes
12–15 asparagus spears
String beans
2 cups julienned carrots
4 garlic cloves

2 onion bouillon cubes

Herbamare
Olive oil

Steam the potatoes, carrots, and string beans for 20 minutes.

Place the steamed vegetables in a baking pan, drizzle with olive oil, and season with pepper, salt (Herbamare), and garlic cloves. Bake for 30 minutes at 175°C/350°F. Remove from oven.

Place string beans and garlic cloves aside. Let pan with potatoes and carrots cool down.

Pierce the veal all over with a fork. Season with salt and pepper and some of the juices from the vegetable pan. Wrap the bacon strips around the veal loin.

Place the veal in the cooled-down pan with the carrots and potatoes. Drizzle some more of the pan juice over the veal.

Place the remaining uncooked vegetables in the pan alongside the potatoes and carrot (namely the cauliflower florets from the head and the trimmed asparagus).

Dissolve the onion bouillon cubes in the water and pour into the dish.

Bake in the oven for 45 minutes at 190°C/375°F.

You can microwave the string beans to reheat when ready to serve. Let the veal sit for 5 minutes after coming out of the oven. Slice and serve with vegetables and gravy.

Leftovers:
If you have leftover veal you can slice it down to make a salad. Clean and chop some romaine lettuce and slice some good-quality Parmesan cheese. Toss the cheese with the romaine, salt, pepper, and Caesar dressing. Add some diced tomato for color. Set out on a plate and arrange the thinly sliced veal on top.

VEAL SIRLOIN WITH CELERY

Start to finish: 105 minutes
Serves 2–4

800g/2 pounds veal sirloin

3 celery stalks
1 cup chopped parsley
1 teaspoon thyme

Salt
Beef bouillon
1 teaspoon garlic powder
Fresh ground pepper
1 cup water

Preheat oven to 200°C/400°F. Thinly slice three celery stalks on the diagonal. Place in a roasting pan and add the parsley, some fresh ground pepper, and the water. Place in the oven to roast for about 40 minutes. While celery is roasting, pierce the veal sirloin all over with a knife and rub down with salt and ground pepper. Season the skin with garlic powder and thyme; rub them in. If using fresh thyme, rub 2 or 3 stems to remove the thyme leaves that you will use. Let marinate for an hour. The liquid in the celery most likely will have evaporated. Remove celery from the oven.

Increase the oven temperature to 220°C/425°F. Add 1 cup of beef bouillon to the celery and place the veal roast in the dish. Bake at 220°C/425°F for 15 to 20 minutes.

Lower oven temperature to 200°C/400°F and continue cooking for 10 minutes. Turn off the oven. Baste the meat with the celery and juices. Depending on taste, let sirloin rest in the still-hot oven a while longer (another 15 minutes and it will still be pink) or remove from oven and let rest for ten minutes. The roast should be pink and tender.

Serve with a nice pasta in tomato sauce.

PIZZA STEAK
Prep time: 30–40 minutes
Serves as many as desired

1 200g ribeye steak per person
Thinly sliced buffalo mozzarella

2 jalapeño peppers

Italian tomato sauce, passata
Herbes de Provençe
Flour

Light olive oil
Butter

Flatten steaks with a mallet, pierce the flesh all over with a fork; season each steak on both sides with a pinch of salt, pepper, and Herbes de Provence.

Lightly flour both sides of the meat.

Slice the hot peppers in half lengthwise. Discard the seeds and dredge the peppers in the excess flour.

Heat 1–2 tablespoons of olive oil and 25g/1 tablespoon of butter in a skillet. Salt the oil.

Fry each steak for 3 minutes per side. The meat edges should get slightly crispy. Place the hot peppers skin-side down in the oil next to the meat.

Remove the meat and place in a baking dish.

Preheat oven to 175°C/350°F. Thinly slice the mozzarella and layer on the steaks, about two slices of mozzarella per steak, then spread a generous tablespoon of your favorite Italian tomato sauce over the cheese on top of the meat.

Place the peppers in the dish next to the meat.

Place dish in the oven to finish off baking to melt the cheese and heat the sauce. This takes 15 to 20 minutes.

BACON PENNETTE
Start to finish: 1 hour
Serves 6

3 slices of turkey bacon

2 cups cherry tomato and basil pasta sauce
2 vine tomatoes
1 zucchini

Pennette (250 g/half a pack)

Passata
Parmesan for grating
Mini mozzarella balls

Preheat oven to 200°C/400°F.

Boil the pasta for 10 minutes in water seasoned with 1 teaspoon of sea salt and 1 tablespoon of olive oil.

While pasta is boiling, deseed the tomatoes and cut into pieces. Clean and chop the zucchini. Quarter the zucchini lengthwise, and then slice into 2-inch pieces. Chop the bacon into pieces.

Drain pasta and place in a shallow casserole dish.

Combine the tomatoes, zucchini, bacon, mini mozzarella balls, and sauce. Season with fresh ground pepper and sea salt.

Stir in up to 6 cups of the passata. Adjust the passata to how dry or moist you want the pasta.

Bake in the oven for 30 minutes.

Remove dish and sprinkle fresh grated Parmesan, about ½ cup, over the dish. Bake in the oven for another ten minutes.

Eat alone or serve with a salad.

GROUND TURKEY AND VEAL PASTA SAUCE

A lighter version of Bolognese sauce.

Start to finish: 2½ hours
Serves 4–6

250g/ ½ lb. ground turkey
250g/ ½ lb. ground veal

2 garlic cloves
1 yellow onion
1 handful chopped fresh basil
1 teaspoon oregano
½ green bell pepper
1 small red pepper

1 chicken bouillon cube
1 teaspoon fennel seeds
Chili flakes (*optional*)
Peppercorns
Salt
1 tube tomato paste
1 can chopped tomatoes
1 tablespoon onion-flavored gravy granules
1 teaspoon sugar (*optional*)

1 cup olive oil

Begin by dicing the peeled garlic cloves, peeled onion, and flesh of the red and green bell peppers. Pour the olive oil into a large saucepan, and salt the oil. Heat the oil on medium. When hot, sauté the fennel seeds, garlic, onion, 8 to 10 peppercorns, basil, oregano, and chili flakes (to taste, I would use 1 teaspoon) in the olive oil for 5 minutes. Add the bell peppers and bouillon cube. Mix well, cover and let simmer for 10 minutes.

Mix in the meats, a drizzle of olive oil, and a dash of salt. Brown the meat. This takes about 15 minutes.

Stir in the tomatoes and the paste, then cover and let simmer for an hour.

After an hour, add the onion granules. Depending on your market, the granules may be labeled as onion flavor gravy granules. If not available, the sauce can be thickened as desired by adding more tomato paste or a teaspoon of flour mixed with ½ cup of cold water. Add a teaspoon of sugar if desired. Let simmer for another half hour or until ready to serve.

Instead of Parmesan, grate some pecorino cheese as a garnish. This adds a flavorful balance to the meat. Pecorino stands up more to blander meats like veal.

Desserts

CRUMBLE CAKE WITH YELLOW SUMMER FRUITS

Start to finish: 90 minutes
Serves 10

8 apples, peeled, cored, and cubed
4 peaches, peeled, pitted, and sliced
4 nectarines, peeled, pitted, and sliced
Flesh and juice of 2 ripe mangoes
Juice of 1 small lemon

4 cloves
¾ cup +1 tablespoon sieved brown sugar, *divided*
White sugar *(optional)*
Nutmeg
1½ cups plain flour

125g/8 tablespoons chilled salted butter

Cook the apples, cloves, tablespoon of brown sugar, and nutmeg in ½ cup of butter. Let cool. Remove the cloves.

Mix the apples with the other fruits, lemon juice, and 2 tablespoons of white sugar (the white sugar is optional and certainly not necessary).

Preheat the oven to 190°C/375°F.

Prepare the crumble topping by rubbing together the 125g/8 tablespoons of chilled butter, ¾ cup of brown sugar, and the flour. You want to rub these ingredients until you get varying pebble-size pieces of mixture.

Place the fruit in a deep baking dish. Spread the crumble over the top. Bake for 30 to 40 minutes.

CHOCOLATE MOUSSE

Prep time: 1 hour
Serves 12

 400–450g quality chocolate
 1 heaping tablespoon heavy cream
 1 vanilla bean pod
 6 large eggs, room temperature, separated
 Powdered sugar
 Pinch of salt

The quality of the chocolate is important. I like a dark Belgian milk chocolate. Heat the chocolate in a bain-marie or large saucepan until it melts. Stir in the beans of the vanilla pod and the cream. Whisk or beat in the egg yolks one at a time. Each yolk is to be mixed in before the next is added. When the last yolk is mixed in, remove from the heat and let cool.

Add a pinch of salt to the egg whites and whip to stiffen. I sparingly sprinkle powdered sugar (probably not more than 2 tablespoons) into the egg whites in intervals. Stiffen into a meringue or as close as you can get.

Fold the egg whites into the now room-temperature chocolate mixture. I like to make one large mousse, but of course individual serving pots can also be used. Pour the chocolate mixture into the desired serving dish and chill.

Topping:
Strawberries, pitted cherries, rose syrup cordial: Place 4 cups of sliced, ripe strawberries in a glass dish. Mix in 2 cups of pitted and coarsely chopped (or halved) cherries. Stir in ¼ to ½ cup rose cordial. Leave to chill until ready to serve as a topping for the chocolate mousse.

FRUIT SALADS

Fruit is as reliable as the ice cream sundae for non-bakers.
Serves 4–6

Blackberry, blueberry, diced mango.

To make when blackberries are in season. Mix 2 cups of each fruit.

Orange slices topped with toasted shredded coconut and chopped mint leaves.

Lightly toast 1 cup of shredded coconut. Peel 4 oranges and slice on the round so you have a cross section of each wedge. Place the orange slices in as flat a layer as possible on a round dish. A few dashes of orange flower water can be poured over the oranges before sprinkling all of the toasted coconut over the orange slices. Garnish with chopped mint leaves.

Strawberries, raspberries, cooked beet, blackberries, mango, rose syrup cordial, and powdered sugar.

I slice my strawberries so that I use only the outer red flesh. The stem and white core are discarded.

> 4 cups of strawberries, sliced
> 3 cups of raspberries
> 1 cooked beetroot, very finely minced
> 2 cups blackberries
> 3 cups diced mango
> 1 cup rose syrup cordial
> Powdered sugar, to sprinkle

Mix all of the fruits in a glass bowl with the beet. Pour in the rose syrup, mix well, add up to a tablespoon of powdered sugar if desired. Mix well. I prepare hours before serving to allow the flavors time to marry or mingle.

MERINGUE MESS
Serves: 1 cup of fruit per person.

White peaches, grilled slices
Olive oil
Mango, diced flesh
Raspberries
Large, prepared meringue
Vanilla ice cream

If the peaches are very ripe, keep the skin to add depth of flavor. Otherwise, peel the peaches. Slice the peaches into ½-centimeter wedges. Lightly brush the wedges with olive oil and grill. When done, mix all the fruits together.

Slice the meringue on the round and place soft vanilla ice cream on the base and pour the fruit on top. Place the top of the meringue on top of the fruit. Other garnishes can be added but I keep it simple. When breaking the meringue to serve, you get a nice mess.

APPLE PIZZA
Start to finish: 60 minutes
Serves 8

6–8 apples
Juice of ½ lemon

Light brown sugar
1 tablespoon vanilla extract
Pinch of salt

All-butter puff pastry

Preheat oven to 220°C/425°F.

Peel, halve, and core apples. Slice thinly and evenly with a mandoline. Place in a bowl and coat with lemon juice, salt, sugar, and vanilla extract. Roll out pastry on the pizza pan. Pinch edges up. Pour apple mixture onto dough and evenly spread out. Reduce oven temperature to 200°C/400°F. Bake the pizza for 40 minutes.

Just as desserts are a perfect end to a meal, they are as well to this part of my story.

We all know sugar, although really good, is not good for you. When living in Africa, I noticed that for a rare sweet treat, children (even my own) were given a sugar cube, not cookies, cakes, or candy. Cringing at the idea that a sugar cube actually tastes good, I eventually tried one to see what all the hype was about. It was really good and further brought home the importance of cultivating a child's palate to embrace balance and taste; it makes the exceptional sweet all the better. Balance makes life all the better.

I strongly feel that healthy eating is not to enable us to live longer on this earth. It is to make sure that we feel good, healthy, and enabled to embrace the highs and manage the lows each day we are here. Good food, what healthy eating can be about, is about feeling good in the here and now. Healthy eating includes thankfulness, awareness, and communion. Let's be *thankful* for what we have. Let's be *aware* of what is good for our loved ones and for ourselves. Let's *not forget* human communion—in so many cultures this is what mealtime is all about—and that there is always enough at the table.

On Death

> Should I have the luxury of knowing when we meet,
> Oh, opportunity
> Then I shall, in my final hours
> Eat!
> The flesh of lobster drenched in salted French butter
> The tail, the claws
> Stuff of my dreams,
> A *crabe farci*, one last fried chicken wing,
> And caviar! . . .
> Otherwise, Death,
> Living is dying
> So, I sample, I savor, I taste and rarely waste
> Yes, so I eat
> Always knowing we will meet.